Handbook for Biblical Studies

Handbook for Biblical Studies

NICHOLAS TURNER

The Westminster Press
Philadelphia

© Nicholas Turner 1982
Maps and ancient scripts © David Turner 1982

Published by The Westminster Press®
Philadelphia, Pennsylvania

PRINTED IN THE UNITED STATES OF AMERICA
9 8 7 6 5 4 3 2 1

Library of Congress Cataloging in Publication Data

Turner, Nicholas.
  Handbook for Biblical studies.

  1. Bible—Handbooks, manuals, etc. 2. Bible—
Dictionaries. 3. Theologians—Biography. I. Title.
BS417.T78   220.6′1   82-7111
ISBN 0-664-24436-X   AACR2

Contents

Nicholas Turner is tutor in Old Testament Studies at St. Stephen's House, Oxford, and lecturer in Old Testament Theology at Keble College, Oxford.

Introduction

It was in my first week at university as a student in Theology, when I had forgotten the meaning of the word 'eschatology' for the third time in the space of only a few days, that I discovered that feeling of despair and utter helplessness in the face of an overwhelming tide of jargon, foreign words and technical terms, which was to recur many times before I had reached my Finals. 'The panic factor' plays a large part in one's years as a student. After all, what can one do when a particular word cannot be found in a regular dictionary, nor a dictionary of the Bible, nor apparently anywhere at all, and yet is used as though everyone ought to, and apparently does, know what it means?

'That's all part of learning: it's good for one,' you might say. But I encountered the problem from the other side as well. Working as a curate in a parish, I tried, if only for half a day a week, to keep up some serious biblical reading. I may have known most of the jargon in my last year of study, but I very soon forgot much of it. How do you remember the different books of Baruch, when you are trying to remember the different Misses Brown? What significance has *Überliefe-rungsgeschichte* when you are visiting someone in hospital or trying to chair a rebellious committee? And to make it worse, one no longer has a college library or a fellow student to turn to for help.

The bulk of this handbook, therefore, consists of a glossary of terms. It is not that theological terms as such are a good thing and ought at all times to be remembered. Some are hideous, grotesque and should never have been invented. But the fact is that writers use them, and one wants to understand what they mean without undue difficulty. The purpose of this book is to make the meaning of these uncommon words accessible as rapidly as possible, so that the reader can move straight to what the writer has to say. Oysters are excellent nourishment; traditionally they are eaten with a little lemon juice or tabasco, accompanied by a Muscadet, but one does also need an efficient oyster-knife to open them quickly and easily.

It is not then the aim of this book to teach. The larger Introductions to the Bible have long articles on historical criticism, its forms over the last two hundred years, the texts it has hypothesized and so on. All well and good. Certainly there are some people who can sit down and learn what these different terms mean and the nuances between them, but it seems equally certain that there are many more who cannot. One learns the terminology as one uses it, or watches other people using it. One can happily begin to learn how to give sound exegesis, without knowing what the word means. Most people do.

As well as technical terms and jargon peculiar to biblical studies, I have included others from a wider context that are frequently used; foreign words that are commonly left untranslated, mainly Hebrew, Greek, Latin and German; brief summaries of books, sources, authors and manuscripts likely to be encountered; and finally several Latin phrases, for, as well as the considerable amount of Latin peculiar to biblical studies, there is also much that is common to any scholarly writing. Annoyingly for many readers, the use of such words appears to be continuing long after the demise of the classical education that made them immediately recognizable.

Since the purpose is to remind rather than to teach, all the definitions have been kept as simple as possible. They are intended to make sense if and when you come across the term in a book: you already have the word in context, so this can be taken as understood. However, 'simple' could mean 'over-simple'. I can but warn the readers; to have included all the ifs and buts, all the possible qualifications, would have defeated the initial purpose through sheer volume.

In addition to the glossary of terms, this handbook contains lists of what I hope will be useful introductory information. It includes, for example, simple chronologies of events, the dating of the books of the Bible, some general features of the languages you will encounter, and brief details of early fathers and modern scholars.

As far as possible the information on the texts follows the consensus of liberal, historical criticism: firstly, because, if and where such a consensus exists, it is that which is relied upon in the great majority of scholarly works; secondly, because a conservative, 'orthodox' approach is considerably less informative. If one is told that Deutero-Isaiah was written about 540 BC by someone other than the 8th century prophet of Jerusalem, one can always 'correct' that view and conform it to tradition; the process does not work the other way round.

This book will not, however, tell you who Jehoshaphat, Jezebel and Jehu were, nor what the Urim and Thummin were used for. These can easily be found elsewhere, for any word within the Bible text itself has been exhaustively covered again and again. Nor does it have a list of the animals mentioned in the Bible. This information is available under dozens of covers. Rather, it is the word or the work *not* found in the standard reference books that can prove so frustratingly elusive, and creates the greatest obstacle to study for all but the initiated.

This book hopes to be that neat, little oyster-knife. In itself a thing of modest worth. But with a certain and precise usefulness.

Compiling such a dictionary can make one an unusually boring person to live with. My thanks therefore go to the people of St Matthew's, Stretford, who allowed me to get started, and to my students at St Stephen's House and Keble College, who took the early drafts. I am also very grateful to those who have helped me sharpen up my definitions or track down others, in particular Dr John Muddiman, Dr Bob Morgan and Mrs Sue Gillingham, and to Miss Rosemary Dawson, who helped me through the final correcting.

Abbreviations of the Books of the Bible

Acts	Acts	Joel	Joel
Am.	Amos	Jn.	John
Bar.	Baruch	I Jn.	I John
I Ch.	I Chronicles	II Jn.	II John
II Ch.	II Chronicles	III Jn.	III John
I Cor.	I Corinthians	Jon.	Jonah
II Cor.	II Corinthians	Jos.	Joshua
Col.	Colossians	Jude	Jude
Dan.	Daniel	I Kg.	I Kings
Deut.	Deuteronomy	II Kg.	II Kings
Ecc.	Ecclesiastes	Lam.	Lamentations
Eph.	Ephesians	Lev.	Leviticus
I Esd.	III (I) Ezra	Lk.	Luke
II Esd.	IV (II) Ezra	I Macc.	I Maccabees
Est.	Esther	II Macc.	II Maccabees
Ex.	Exodus	Mal.	Malachi
Ezek.	Ezekiel	Mic.	Micah
Ezr.	Ezra	Mk.	Mark
Gal.	Galatians	Mt.	Matthew
Gen.	Genesis	Nah.	Nahum
Hab.	Habakkuk	Neh.	Nehemiah
Hag.	Haggai	Num.	Numbers
Heb.	Hebrews	Ob.	Obadiah
Hos.	Hosea	I Pet.	I Peter
Is.	Isaiah	II Pet.	II Peter
Jas.	James	Phil.	Philippians
Jdt.	Judith	Phm.	Philemon
Jer.	Jeremiah	Prov.	Proverbs
Jg.	Judges	Pss.	Psalms
Job	Job	Rev.	Revelation

Rom.	Romans	II Th.	II Thessalonians
Rt.	Ruth	I Tim.	I Timothy
I Sam.	I Samuel	II Tim.	II Timothy
II Sam.	II Samuel	Tit.	Titus
Sir.	Sirach	Tob.	Tobit
S. of S.	Song of	Wis.	Wisdom
	Solomon	Zech.	Zechariah
I Th.	I Thessalonians	Zeph.	Zephaniah

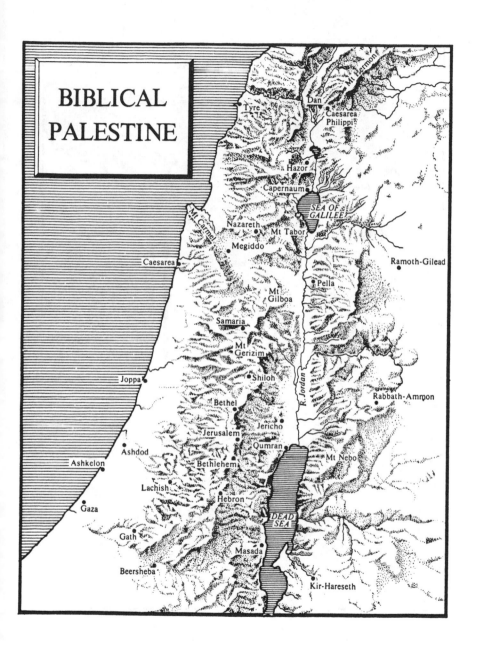

BIBLICAL PALESTINE

Tyre

Dan

Caesarea Philippi

Mt Hermon

Hazor

Capernaum

SEA OF GALILEE

Mt Carmel

Nazareth

Mt Tabor

Megiddo

Caesarea

Ramoth-Gilead

Mt Gilboa

Pella

Samaria

Mt Gerizim

Shiloh

Joppa

R. Jordan

Rabbath-Ammon

Bethel

Jericho

Jerusalem

Qumran

Ashdod

Mt Nebo

Ashkelon

Bethlehem

Lachish

Hebron

Gaza

DEAD SEA

Gath

Masada

Beersheba

Kir-Hareseth

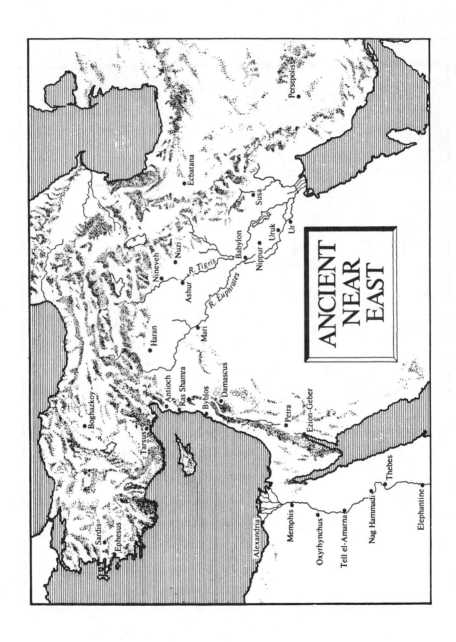

The Essential Dates

Most dictionaries and study Bibles have a full chronology of events, but these are inevitably confusing to the beginner or the part-time student. Below therefore is a simple chronology and first, in case that is still too complex, an even simpler one. Because of the difficulty of relating one ancient calendar to another, some even of the best assured dates can differ by one year according to the method of calculation; for example, one can find the fall of Jerusalem recorded as 587 BC or 586.

Super-Simple Chronology

c. 1800 BC	Abraham
c. 1250	The Exodus
c. 1000	David captures Jerusalem
c. 930	Division of the Kingdoms
c. 850	Elijah
721	Fall of Samaria
621	Josiah's reform
587	Fall of Jerusalem
c. 400	Ezra brings the Law to Jerusalem
167	Start of the Maccabean revolt
63	Pompey captures Jerusalem
30 AD	The Crucifixion
70	Fall of Jerusalem
135	Defeat of Bar-Kochba

Simple Chronology

c. 1800 BC	Abraham
c. 1250	The Exodus
c. 1220	Conquest of Canaan under Joshua
c. 1125 BC	Victory of Deborah and Barak at Taanach
c. 1050	Destruction of Shiloh by the Philistines
c. 1000	David captures Jerusalem from the Jebusites
c. 930	Rebellion of Jeroboam I; division of the Kingdoms
c. 875	Foundation of Samaria by Omri
c. 850	Elijah
c. 740	Call of Isaiah; expansion of the Assyrian Empire
721	Fall of Samaria; end of the Northern Kingdom
701	Sennacherib invades Judah
621	Josiah's reform and the discovery of the 'Book of the Law'
612	Destruction of Nineveh, capital of the Assyrian Empire
609	Death of Josiah at Megiddo, while opposing Pharaoh Neco
598	First capture of Jerusalem by the Babylonians
587	Fall of Jerusalem and destruction of the Temple
581	Further deportations to Babylonia
538	Edict of Cyrus and first return of the Exiles
520	Preaching of Haggai and Zechariah
515	Second Temple completed
c. 445	Nehemiah's first mission to Jerusalem
c. 400	Ezra brings the Law to Jerusalem
332	Conquest of Palestine by Alexander the Great
198	Judaea comes under Seleucid rule
167	Beginning of the Maccabean revolt
164	Restoration of sacrifice in the Temple
142	End of Seleucid rule; Simon high priest
128	John Hyrcanus conquers Samaria
63	Pompey captures Jerusalem
37	Herod the Great gains control of Jerusalem
30 AD	The Crucifixion (if AD 30 is correct, the date is Friday, 7th April)
c. 37	Martyrdom of Stephen

c. 43   Paul and Barnabas at Antioch
    51   Paul at Corinth
    58   Paul arrested at Jerusalem
    62 AD Martyrdom of James, brother of the Lord, at Jerusalem
    64   Martyrdom of Peter (and Paul?) at Rome
    66   Beginning of the Jewish revolt
    70   Fall of Jerusalem and destruction of the Temple by the Romans
    73   Fall of Masada
c. 85   Rabbinic council at Jamnia; break with the Church
  132   Beginning of the second Jewish revolt
  135   Defeat of Simon Bar Kochba by the Romans

Archaeological Periods in Palestine

Palaeolithic – Old Stone Age	250,000–10,000 BC
Mesolithic – Middle Stone Age	10,000– 7500
Neolithic – New Stone Age	7500– 4000
Chalcolithic	4000– 3100
Early Bronze Age	3100– 2200
Middle Bronze Age	2200– 1500
Late Bronze Age	1500– 1200
Iron Age 1★	1200– 1000
Iron Age 2★	1000– 800
Iron Age 3★	800– 587
Persian Period	587– 332
Hellenistic Period	332– 63
Roman Period	BC 63– 324 AD
Byzantine Period	324– 640
Early Arab Period	640– 1099
Crusader Period	1099– 1291

★ Sometimes simplified to: Iron Age 1 1200–900 BC
                             Iron Age 2   900–600

Empires, Dynasties and Rulers

From the days of Sargon the Great of Akkad (*c.* 2350 BC), mighty kings, emperors and governors held sway across vast stretches of the ancient Near East, and lesser or less fortunate rulers made treaties or surrendered. Lists of these men can be long and confusing, but as elsewhere I follow the principle that some information is better than none at all.

The dating of the reigns of these ancient rulers is a complex problem, and, particularly in the case of the kings of Israel and Judah, more than one chronology has been proposed and is in current use. These dates for all their apparent precision cannot therefore be certain.

The Kings of Israel and Judah

The United Kingdom
1030–1010 BC Saul
1010–970   David
970–931   Solomon

Israel		*Judah*	
931–910	Jeroboam I	931–913	Rehoboam
910–909	Nadab	913–911	Abijah (Abijam)
909–886	Baasha	911–870	Asa
886–885	Elah	870–848	Jehoshaphat
7 days	Zimri	848–841	Jehoram
885–874	Omri	841	Ahaziah
874–853	Ahab	841–835	Athaliah
853–852	Ahaziah	835–796	Joash
852–841	Jehoram	796–781	Amaziah

Israel		Judah	
841–814	Jehu	781–740	Uzziah (Azariah)
814–801	Jehoahaz	740–736	Jotham
801–786	Joash	736–716	Ahaz (Jehoahaz)
786–746	Jeroboam II	716–687	Hezekiah
746–745	Zechariah	687–642	Manasseh
745	Shallum	642–640	Amon
745–738	Menahem	640–609	Josiah
738–737	Pekahiah	609	Jehoahaz (Shallum)
737–732	Pekah	609–598	Jehoiakim (Eliakim)
732–721	Hoshea	598	Jehoiachin (Jeconiah)
Fall of Samaria		598–587	Zedekiah (Mattaniah)
		Fall of Jerusalem	

Pharaohs and Kings of Egypt

DYNASTY		PHARAOH
Old Kingdom		
Ist	3100–2900 BC	Traditional founder: Menes
IInd	2900–2780	
IIIrd	2780–2680	(The Stepped Pyramid of Djoser)
IVth	2680–2560	(The Great Pyramid of Cheops)
Vth	2560–2420	
VIth	2420–2260	
First Intermediate Period		
VII–XIth		
	2260–1990	
Middle Kingdom		
XIIth	1990–1780	
Second Intermediate Period		
XIII–XVIIth		
	1780–1552	The Hyksos rulers

8

New Kingdom

XVIIIth	1552–1306	Amosis	1552–1527
		Amenhotep I	1527–1507
		(or: Amenophis)	
		Thutmosis I	1507–1494
		Thutmosis II	1494–1490
		Thutmosis III	1490–1436
		Amenhotep II	1438–1412
		Thutmosis IV	1412–1403
		Amenhotep III	1403–1364
		Amenhotep IV	1364–1347
		(or: Akhenaton)	
XIXth	1306–1200	Sethos I	1305–1290
		Rameses II	1290–1224
		Marniptah	1224–1211
XXth	1185–1069	Rameses III	1183–1152

Later Rulers

XXIst	1069–935	Psusennis II	967–962
	(Tanite)		
XXIInd	935–725	Shishak	935–914
		Osorkon I	914–874
XXIIIrd	759–715		
XXIVth	715–709	Bocchoris	715–709
XXVth	716–664	Shabako	710–696
	(Ethiopian)	Shebteko	696–685
		Tirhakah	685–664
XXVIth	664–525	Psammethichus I	664–610
	(Saitic)	Neco II	609–594
		Psammetichus II	594–589
		Apries	589–570
		(or: Hophra)	
		Amasis	570–526
XXVIIth	525–401	The Persian kings	
XXVIII–XXXth			
	401–343	(Independent)	
332	Conquest by Alexander the Great		

323–285 Ptolemy I Lagi
285–246 Ptolemy II Philadelphus

9

246–221	Ptolemy III Euergetes
221–203	Ptolemy IV Philopator
203–181	Ptolemy V Epiphanes
181–146	Ptolemy VI Philometor
146–117	Ptolemy VII Physcon

Earliest Empires of Mesopotamia and Asia Minor

	DYNASTY OR EMPIRE	RULER	
Mesopotamia			
2850–2350	Sumer: Early Dynastic period		
2350–2180	Akkadian Empire	Sargon the Great	*c.* 2350
2060–1950	3rd Dynasty of Ur	Hammurabi	1728–1686
1830–1530	1st Babylonian Dynasty	Zimrilin	1730–1697
1750–1697	Mari Age		
1500–1370	Kingdom of Mitanni		
Asia Minor			
1650–1500	Old Hittite Empire	Labarnas	*c.* 1600
		Hattusilis I	*c.* 1575
		Mursilis I	*c.* 1550
1400–1200	New Hittite Empire	Shuppiluliuma	1375–1335
		Muwattalis	1306–1282
		Hattusilis II	1275–1250

Later Rulers in Mesopotamia and Asia Minor

Syria
Rezon	*c.* 950 BC
Ben-hadad I	880–842

Hazael   842–806 BC
Ben-hadad II   c. 800
Rezin   740–732
Fall of Damascus

Assyrian Kings

1365–1330 Ashuruballit	884–859 Ashurnasirpal II
1308–1275 Adadnirari I	858–824 Shalmaneser III
1274–1245 Shalmaneser I	810–783 Adadnirari III
1245–1209 Tukulti-Ninurta I	782–772 Shalmaneser IV
1132–1115 Ashurreshishi I	745–727 Tiglath-Pileser III
1115–1077 Tiglath-Pileser I	726–722 Shalmaneser V
1049–1031 Ashurnasirpal I	722–705 Sargon II
1030–1019 Shalmaneser II	704–681 Sennacherib
1012– 972 Ashurrabi I	680–669 Esarhaddon
966– 935 Tiglath-Pileser II	668–629 Ashurbanipal
935– 913 Ashurdan II	626–612 Shinsharishkun
912– 892 Adadnirari II	Fall of Nineveh
891– 884 Tukulti-Ninurta II	

Neo-Babylonian Kings

625–605 BC Nebupolassar
605–562   Nebuchadnezzar
561–560   Evilmerodach
556–539   Nabonidus
Fall of Babylon

Persian Kings

559–530 BC	Cyrus	404–358	Artaxerxes II
530–522	Cambyses		Mnemon
522–486	Darius I	358–338	Artaxerxes III
486–464	Xerxes		Ochus
	(Ahasuerus)	336–330	Darius III
464–423	Artaxerxes I		Codomannus
	Longimanus	Conquest by Alexander the
423–404	Darius II	Great
	Nothus		

11

Seleucid Kings

312–280 BC	Seleucus I Nicator	163–162	Antiochus V Eupator
280–261	Antiochus I Soter	162–150	Demetrius I Soter
261–246	Antiochus II Theos	150–145	Alexander Balas
246–226	Seleucus II Callinicus	145–138	Demetrius II Nicator
226–223	Seleucus III Soter Ceraunos	145–142	Antiochus VI Epiphanes Dionysus
223–187	Antiochus III the Great	138–129	Antiochus VII Sidetes
187–175	Seleucus IV Philopator	129–125	Demetrius II (again)
175–163	Antiochus IV Epiphanes		

Later Rulers of Palestine

Hasmoneans

166–160 BC	Judas Maccabeus	103–76	Alexander Jannaeus
160–142	Jonathan	76–67	Salome Alexandra
142–134	Simon		
134–104	John Hyrcanus	67–63	Aristobulus II
		63–40	Hyrcanus II
104–103	Aristobulus I	40–37	Antigonus Mattathias

Herodians

37– 4 BC	Herod the Great
BC 4– 6 AD	Archelaus, ethnarch of Judaea
BC 4–39 AD	Herod Antipas, tetrarch of Galilee and Perea
BC 4–34 AD	Philip, tetrarch of Trachonitis, Batanea etc.
37–44	Herod Agrippa I
53–*c.*100	Herod Agrippa II

The Roman Empire

Emperors

BC 37–14 AD Augustus	69– 79 Vespasian
14–37 Tiberius	79– 81 Titus
37–41 Caligula	81– 96 Domitian
41–54 Claudius	96– 98 Nerva
54–68 Nero	98–117 Trajan
68–69 Galba – Otho –	117–138 Hadrian
Vitellius	

Procurators in Judaea and Palestine

6– 9 AD Coponius	*c.* 46–48 Tiberius
9–12 M. Ambibulus	Alexander
12–15 Annius Rufus	48–52 Ventidius
15–26 Valerius Gratus	Cumanus
26–36 Pontius Pilate	52–60 Antonius Felix
36–37 Marcellus	60–62 Porcius Festus
37–41 Herennius Capito	62–64 Clodius Albinus
41–*c.* 46 Cuspius Fadus	64–66 Gessius Florus

Dating of the Books

It is not possible to give a straightforward chronological table of the books of the Bible. Some of the earliest books have late additions. Some of the latest contain early traditions. Nearly all have been edited later. Furthermore, while some books can claim a virtually assured date, others attract considerable disagreement; to take one example, James is generally reckoned to be the earliest book of the New Testament, but some see it as the latest.

Nevertheless it is better to start with a framework that can be altered later, or even entirely rejected, than to have none at all; the books are listed below as far as possible in chronological order. As you get to know a book better, you will be better able to judge why it should be dated earlier or later, and which other works it should be linked with. And with still better knowledge, you may approach the happy state of scholarly 'openness', seeing the possible validity of several options.

The Old Testament

10th cent. BC	J – Yahwist Source
	Succession Narrative
	Joseph Story
9th cent.	Elijah and Elisha Cycles
8th cent.	E – Elohist Source
	Amos
	Hosea
	1st Isaiah
	Micah

7th cent. BC	Proverbs chs. 10–29	
	Zephaniah	
	Deuteronomic Code (621 BC)	
	Nahum	
	Habakkuk	
6th cent.	*Early Exile*	Jeremiah
		Obadiah
		Lamentations
		Deuteronomic History
	Late Exile	Ezekiel
		H – Holiness Code
		2nd Isaiah
	Restoration	Haggai (520)
		1st Zechariah (520)
		3rd Isaiah
5th cent.	P – Priestly Source	
	Job	
	Proverbs chs. 1–9	
	Malachi	
4th cent.	Chronicles – Ezra – Nehemiah	
	Ruth	
	Jonah	
	Joel	
3rd cent.	Isaiah Apocalypse	
	2nd Zechariah	
	Ecclesiastes	
	Esther	
	Song of Solomon	
2nd cent.	Tobit	
	Sirach	
	Daniel (164)	
	Judith	
	I Maccabees	
	Additions to Esther and Daniel	
1st cent.	II Maccabees	
	Wisdom	

- Current scholarship is tending to date the early material later. How long this will last and how much influence it will have on less specialized literature is hard to judge.
- All the pre-exilic prophets have post-exilic additions,

15

which have a marked effect on the overall character of their work.

● Some of the Psalms date back to the early monarchy, perhaps even earlier; others may be from the Maccabean period; however their compilation is generally set about 350 BC.

The New Testament

40s AD	James	70s	Matthew
	Q Sayings Collection		Luke – Acts
50s	I Thessalonians		John
	II Thessalonians	80s	Ephesians
	I Corinthians		Jude
	II Corinthians		I John
	Galatians		II & III John
	Romans	90s	II Timothy
60s	Colossians		I Timothy
	Philippians		Titus
	Mark		II Peter
	I Peter		
	Revelation		
	Hebrews		

● With the exception of the pauline/deutero-pauline works, the sequence is on the whole agreed, but earlier scholars extended it into the 2nd century, while some recent research shortens it, to end in the 80s or even 60s.
● The Gospels in particular have a long period of tradition behind them, going back in oral form to the 30s, which makes the dating of the final work that much less certain.
● The key event against which scholars relate nearly all the works, except the genuine letters of Paul, is the fall of Jerusalem in AD 70.

The Jewish Calendar

MONTH			FESTIVAL	
POST–EXILIC BABYLONIAN NAME (Pre-exilic Canaanite name)			HEBREW NAME (Greek – English names)	
1 NISAN (Abib)	Mar/Apr	14th	PESSAH (Pascha – Passover)	Ex. 12.1ff
		14th–21st	MAZZOTH (Azyma – Unleavened Bread)	Ex. 12.15ff
2 IYYAR (Ziv)	Apr/May			
3 SIVAN	May/Jun	6th	SHAVUOTH (Pentecostes – Pentecost)	Lev. 23.15ff
4 TAMMUZ	Jun/Jul			
5 AB	Jul/Aug			
6 ELUL	Aug/Sep			
7 TISHRI (Ethanim)	Sep/Oct	1st	ROSH HA-SHANAH (Semasia – Trumpets/New Year)	Num. 29.1ff
		10th	YOM KIPPUR (Exilasmos – Day of Atonement)	Lev. 16.1ff
		15th–21st	SUKKOTH (Skenopegie – Tabernacles)	Lev. 23.34ff
8 MARCHESVAN (Bul)	Oct/Nov			
9 CHISLEV	Nov/Dec	25th	HANUKKAH (Encaenia – Dedication)	I Macc. 4.52ff
10 TEBETH	Dec/Jan			
11 SHEBAT	Jan/Feb			
12 ADAR	Feb/Mar	14th–15th	PURIM (Phrurae – Purim)	Est. 9.20ff

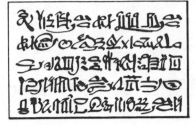

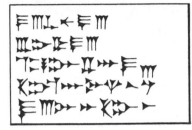

EXAMPLES OF ANCIENT SCRIPTS
(Left to right and top to bottom)
Hieroglyphic, from Egypt, 28th cent. BC; Hieratic, from
Egypt, 13th cent. BC; Pictographic, from Mesopotamia, 31st
cent. BC; Cuneiform, from Ugarit, 15th cent. BC; Archaic
Hebrew, from Jerusalem, 8th cent. BC; Square Hebrew, from
Qumran, 1st cent. AD; Greek Uncial, 4th cent. AD.

The Hebrew Alphabet

		TRANS-LITERATION	MODERN CURSIVE	ARCHAIC	NUMERICAL VALUE
Aleph	א	'			1
Beth	בּ	b			2
	ב	v, bh, b			
Gimel	ג	g			3
	ג	gh, g			
Daleth	דּ	d			4
	ד	dh, d			
He	ה	h			5
Waw	ו	w			6
Zayin	ז	z			7
Heth	ח	ch, ḥ			8
Teth	ט	t, ṭ			9
Yodh	י	y			10
Kaph	כ	k			20
	כ ך	kh, k			
Lamed	ל	l			30
Mem	מ ם	m			40
Nun	נ ן	n			50
Samek	ס	s			60
Ayin	ע	'			70
Pe	פ	p			80
	פ ף	f, ph, p			
Sade	צ ץ	ts, z, ṣ			90
Qoph	ק	q, ḳ			100
Resh	ר	r			200
Shin	שׁ	sh, š			300
(Sin)	שׂ	s, ś			
Tau	תּ	t			400
	ת	th, t			

Vowel Points

Qames	ֹהָ	ָ	â,	ā
Pathah		ַ		a
Sere	ֵי	ֵ	ê,	ē
Seghol		ֶ		e
Hireq	ִי	ִ	î,	i
Holem	ֹו	ֹ	ô,	ō
Qames-Hatuph		ָ		o
Sureq	וּ		û	
Qibbus		ֻ		u

(Simple) Shewa	ְ	ᵉ
Hateph-Pathah	ֲ	ᵃ
Hateph-Seghol	ֱ	ᵉ
Hateph-Qames	ֳ	ᵒ

The Greek Alphabet

	CAPITAL	SMALL	TRANS- LITERATION	ARCHAIC	NUMERICAL VALUE
Alpha	A	α	a	A	1
Beta	B	β	b	ß	2
Gamma	Γ	γ	g	⌐	3
Delta	Δ	δ	d	▷	4
Epsilon	E	ε	e	⋦	5
Zeta	Z	ζ	z	I	7
Eta	H	η	ē, ee	⊟	8
Theta	Θ	θ	th	⊗	9
Iota	I	ι	i	I	10
Kappa	K	κ	k	K	20
Lambda	Λ	λ	l	∧	30
Mu	M	μ	m	⋀	40
Nu	N	ν	n	∿	50
Xi	Ξ	ξ	x	Ⅎ	60
Omicron	O	o	o	O	70
Pi	Π	π	p	Γ	80
Rho	P	ρ	r	D	100
Sigma	Σ	σ,ς	s	⟨	200
Tau	T	τ	t	T	300
Upsilon	Y	υ	u, y	V	400
Phi	Φ	φ	ph, f	Φ	500
Chi	X	χ	ch	+	600
Psi	Ψ	ψ	ps	Ψ	700
Omega	Ω	ω	ō, o	∿	800

Smooth breathing – '
Rough breathing (h) – '

Comma   – ,
Semi-colon   – ·
Full stop   – .
Question mark   – ;

The Problems of Foreign Words

Plurals

Another pitfall, over and above the meaning of Hebrew, Greek, Latin and German words themselves, is the variety of their plural forms. For full details a grammar should, of course, be consulted; the following lists are meant only as a very simple, and by no means comprehensive, guideline to the forms most often encountered.

Hebrew

Masculine		Add **–im**	
Feminine	**–ah**	→ **–oth**	

Greek

Masculine		**–os** → **–oi**	2nd Declension
Feminine	**–a,**	**–e** → **–ai**	1st Declension
Neuter		**–on** → **–a**	2nd Declension
Neuter		**–a** → **–ata**	3rd Declension

Latin

Masculine	**–us** → **–i**	2nd Declension
Feminine	**–a** → **–ae**	1st Declension
Neuter	**–um** → **–a**	2nd Declension
M. & F.	**–ex** → **–ices**	3rd Declension

German

Common	No change	1st Declension
Common	Add **– e**	2nd Declension
Common	Add **– er**	3rd Declension
Common	Add **– en,** **–n**	4th Declension

Transliteration

Hebrew, and to a lesser extent Greek, being written in different scripts to our own, present particular problems of transliteration into English. Is it obvious the 'Ychuda' is in fact the Hebrew name more commonly written 'Judah', or that if the word *chesed* is not listed in a theological word book under C, one should look under H?

Though there is an increasing consensus in scholarly works and the use of diacritical signs is of considerable help where the printing allows it, there are still notable variations between current works, between works of this century and the last, and between Jewish and Christian books. Some of the most common alternatives are listed below; this is not intended to be a complete analysis, simply a guide to the recognition of those difficult words so often left untranslated. Evidently, the best course is to learn the basics of both languages, but that is advice not every student may care to take.

Hebrew
- The script being merely consonantal, vowel sounds are not represented by letters, and can change dramatically with different forms of a word, and so cannot always be relied upon for recognition.
- English has not the same range of gutturals. Thus in particular, **ch** can be written **h**, and **q** can be **k**, or vice versa.
- Six consonants, **b, g, d, k, p, t**, are softened when not at the beginnings of words. This is usually marked by the addition of an **h**, or by a line underneath, though quite often the consonant is left unchanged. Two of these, **b** and **p**, can also be changed to entirely different letters, **v** and **f** respectively.
- Most of the consonants can be doubled within words: this is not always shown.
- **H** is occasionally omitted from the beginning and more often from the end of words.

Greek

• Many Greek words were taken over into Latin, and some that did not exist in the classical world but are made up from Greek roots have been Latinized on their way into English. In particular, the ending **−os** can become **−us**, **k** can become **c**, **ai** and **oi** can become **ae** and **oe**, and other diphthongs can be reduced to the second of the two vowels e.g. **ei** to **i**.

• Both **u** and **y** are used to transliterate Upsilon.

• Iota, particularly at the beginning of a word, can become **j** or **y**, as well as **i**.

Theological Who's Who

Unfamiliar names thrown casually about by those on the inside can often have an even more upsetting effect upon the beginner or amateur than technical jargon. The biographical notes below should help you at least to spell their names correctly and to place them in the right century and context.

The first section lists fathers of the early Church, several heretics and a few Jewish writers whom you may encounter in biblical, usually New Testament, studies. Some are in themselves of little importance: they simply record a version or tradition of the text.

The second section lists modern scholars, including some from the Reformation era, whose hypotheses or seminal work may be quoted, approvingly or otherwise, by others. Of compiling such a list there can be no end, but comprehensiveness has to be balanced with usefulness.

The Early Period

Dates are AD unless specified.
Acacius d. 366   Arian bishop of Caesarea until deposed.
Adamantius early 4th cent.   Greek anti-Gnostic writer.
Akiba *c.* 50–132   Jewish Rabbi, who actively supported Bar Kochba's revolt.
Alexander d. 328   Bishop of Alexandria; anti-Arian.
Ambrose *c.* 399–97   Bishop of Milan; autonomy of the Church.
Ambrosiaster 4th cent.   Name given to the author of a set of Latin commentaries on Paul's epistles.
Ammonius Saccas *c.* 175–242   Founder of Neo-

25

Platonism, from Alexandria; formerly reckoned to have devised the Ammonian Sections.

Amphilochius *c.* 340–95   Bishop of Iconium; related to the Cappadocian Fathers.

Aphraates early 4th cent.   First of the Syrian Fathers.

Apollinarius *c.* 310–*c.* 390   Christological heretic, from Syria.

Aristides 2nd cent.   Philosopher and apologist, from Athens.

Arius *c.* 250–*c.* 336   The great subordinationist heretic.

Athanasius *c.* 296–373   Bishop of Alexandria; opponent of Arius.

Athenagoras 2nd cent.   Greek apologist.

Augustine 354–430   Bishop of Hippo; greatest of the Latin Fathers; *City of God*.

Basil the Great *c.* 330–79   One of the three Cappadocian Fathers.

Carpocrates 2nd cent.   Gnostic teacher, from Alexandria.

Cassian, John *c.* 360–435   Monastic founder.

Chromatius d. 407   Bishop of Aquileia, N. Italy; homilies on Matthew.

Chrysostom, John *c.* 347–407   Patriarch of Constantinople; renowned preacher.

Clement of Alexandria *c.* 150–*c.* 215   Christian gnosticism; *Stromateis*.

Clement of Rome *fl. c.* 96   Bishop; one of the Apostolic Fathers.

Cyprian d. 258   Bishop of Carthage, N. Africa.

Cyril of Alexandria d. 444   Bishop; opponent of Nestorius.

Cyril of Jerusalem *c.* 315–86   Bishop; *Catechetical Lectures*.

Didymus the Blind *c.* 313–98   Alexandrian theologian and teacher.

Diodore d. *c.* 390   Bishop of Tarsus; Antiochene theologian.

Dionysius the Great d. *c.* 264   Bishop of Alexandria.

Ephraem Syrus *c.* 306–73   Major Syrian Father.

Epiphanius *c.* 315–403   Bishop of Salamis; *Refutations of all the Heresies*.

Eusebius   c. 260–c. 340   Bishop of Caesarea; *Ecclesiastical History*.

Eustathius   d. c. 337   Bishop of Antioch; anti-Arian.

Euthalius   4th cent.   Reputed author of the Euthalian Apparatus.

Fastidius   early 5th cent.   British Pelagian writer.

Gamaliel   early 1st cent.   Jewish Rabbi; grandson of Hillel.

Gaudentius   d. 406   Bishop of Brescia; preacher.

Gregory of Elvira   d. 392   Bishop; allegorical exegete.

Gregory of Nazianzus   329–89   Bishop; one of the three Cappadocian Fathers.

Gregory of Nyssa   c. 330–c. 395   Cappadocian Father; brother of Basil.

Gregory Thaumaturgus   c. 213–c. 270   Bishop of Neocaesarea; disciple of Origen.

Hegesippus   2nd cent.   Church historian; *Hypomnemata*.

Heracleon   fl. c. 145–80   Gnostic teacher; disciple of Valentinus.

Hesychius of Jerusalem   d. after 451   Bible commentator of the Alexandrian school.

Hieronymous   See JEROME.

Hilary of Poitiers   c. 315–67   The 'Athanasius of the West'.

Hillel   late 1st cent. BC   Early Jewish Rabbi, who opposed Shammai; liberal interpretation of the Law.

Hippolytus of Rome   c. 170–c. 236   Ecclesiastical and liturgical writer; possible anti-pope.

Ignatius of Antioch   c. 35–107   Bishop; one of the Apostolic Fathers, writer of seven epistles.

Irenaeus   c. 130–c. 200   Bishop of Lyon; *Adversus Omnes Haereses*.

Jerome   c. 342–420   Translator of the Vulgate.

Johanan ben Zaccai   c. 1–c. 80   Jewish Rabbi; disciple of Hillel.

Josephus, Flavius   c. 37–c. 100   Jewish historian; *The Jewish War*, *Antiquities of the Jews*.

Judah   135–217   Jewish Rabbi, known simply as 'Rabbi'; compiler of the Mishnah.

Julius Africanus   c. 160–c. 240   From Palestine; *History of the World*.

Justin Martyr *c.*100–*c.*165 Major apologist; *First & Second Apology, Dialogue with Trypho.*
Juvencus early 4th cent. Latin poet who wrote a harmony of the gospels in hexameters.
Leo d. 461 Pope; *Tome.*
Lucian of Antioch d. 312 Reviser of the Greek text of the Bible.
Lucifer d. 370 Bishop of Cagliari; anti-Arian.
Manes or **Mani** *c.*216–76 Founder of Manichaeism, from Persia.
Marcion d. *c.* 160 Heretic who rejected the Old Testament and devised his own canon.
Meir *c.* 110–*c.* 175 Jewish Rabbi; one of the leading Tannaim.
Melitius d. 381 Bishop of Antioch.
Melito d. *c.* 190 Bishop of Sardis; *Peri Pascha.*
Methodius of Olympus d. *c.* 311 Bishop; opponent of Origen's thought.
Nestorius d. *c.* 451 Heresiarch from Syria, who argued for two persons in Christ.
Nonnus of Panopolis d. *c.* 431 Wrote a paraphrase of the 4th Gospel.
Novatian 3rd cent. Founder of the rigorist sect of Novatianists; elected anti-pope in 251.
Optatus *fl.* 370 Bishop of Milevus, N. Africa; early opponent of the Donatists.
Origen *c.* 185–*c.* 254 Greatest of the Greek Fathers, working in Alexandria and Caesarea; *De Principiis, Contra Celsum.*
Orosius early 5th cent. Colleague of Augustine in the fight against Pelagianism.
Pamphilus *c.* 240–309 Teacher at Caesarea; wrote an apology in favour of Origen.
Papias *c.* 60–130 Bishop of Hierapolis, Asia Minor; wrote on the origins of the gospels.
Paulinus 353–431 Bishop of Nola, Spain; poet.
Pelagius *fl.* late 4th cent. The great British heretic, arguing that man can make the first, vital step towards his own salvation.
Peter of Alexandria d. 311 Bishop and martyr.

Philo *c.* 20 BC–*c.* AD 50   Jewish exegete from Alexandria, noted for allegorical interpretation.

Philoxenus *c.* 440–523   Monophysite bishop who commissioned the Syriac version of the New Testament named after him.

Plotinus *c.* 205–70   Major Neo-Platonist theologian and mystic, teaching in Rome.

Polycarp *c.* 69–*c.* 155   Bishop of Smyrna, Asia Minor; martyr and one of the Apostolic Fathers.

Porphyry *c.* 232–*c.* 303   Neo-Platonist philosopher and vigorous anti-Christian.

Priscillian d. 386   Bishop of Avila, Spain; executed as a heretic.

Proclus d. 446   Patriarch of Constantinople.

Proclus 411–85   Neo-Platonist teacher; one of the last masters of the Athens Academy.

Rufinus *c.* 345–410   Monk and historian; translator of the Greek Fathers into Latin.

Serapion d. 362   Bishop of Thmuis, Egypt; friend of Athanasius.

Shammai late 1st cent. BC   Early Jewish Rabbi, who opposed Hillel; strict interpretation of the Law.

Socrates *c.* 380–450   Greek church historian.

Sozomon early 5th cent.   Palestinian church historian.

Sulpicius Severus *c.* 360–*c.* 420   Historian and hagiographer from Gaul.

Tatian *fl.* 160   Apologist; encratite; compiler of the *Diatessaron*.

Tertullian *c.* 160–*c.* 225   African; the 'Father of Latin theology'; a rigorist.

Theodore of Mopsuestia *c.* 350–428   Bishop; Antiochene theologian.

Theodoret *c.* 393–*c.* 466   Bishop of Cyrrhus, Syria; one of the principle Antiochene theologians.

Theodotus of Byzantium 2nd cent.   Founder of an adoptionist sect.

Theophilus d. *c.* 180   Bishop of Antioch; apologist.

Tyconius d. *c.* 400   Donatist; *Liber Regularum*.

Valentinus 2nd cent.   The major Gnostic theologian, from Egypt; founder of the Valentinian sect.

Victorinus of Pettau d. *c.* 304 Bishop; earliest known exegete of the Latin Church.
Victorinus of Rome 4th cent. African; Christian Neo-Platonist.
Yehuda See JUDAH.

Modern Scholars

Aland, Kurt 1915– German; NT Greek text.
Albright, William F. 1891–1971 American; OT archaeologist.
Alt, Albrecht 1883–1956 German; OT historian.
Aulen, Gustav 1879–1978 Swedish bishop; *Christus Victor.*
Barr, James 1924– In Oxford, OT; philology and hermeneutics.
Barrett, Charles K. 1917– English; NT commentaries.
Barth, Karl 1886–1968 German Swiss; leader of Neo-Orthodox Theology.
Bauer, Walter 1877–1960 German; NT lexicographer.
Baur, Ferdinand C. 1792–1860 German, NT; Hegelian; founder of historical theology.
Bornkamm, Günther 1905– German, NT; *Jesus, Paul.*
Bousset, Wilhelm 1865–1920 German, NT; one of the founders of the Religionsgeschichtliche Schule.
Bruce, Frederick F. 1910– Scottish; NT history.
Brunner, Emil 1889–1965 Swiss Protestant theologian; opponent of Barth.
Buber, Martin 1878–1965 Austrian; Jewish philosopher.
Bultmann, Rudolf 1884–1976 German, NT; demythologization.
Calvin, John 1509–64 From Geneva; leading Reformation theologian.
Childs, Brevard S. 1923– American, OT; canonical criticism.
Conzelmann, Hans 1915– German, NT; Luke's concept of time.
Cullmann, Oscar 1902– French, NT; development of

salvation history in the early Church.

Davidson, Andrew B. 1831–1902 Scottish Hebraist.

Deissmann, Adolf 1866–1937 German; identified NT as Koine Greek.

De Vaux, Roland 1904–71 French; OT archaeologist; leader of the team which worked on the Dead Sea Scrolls.

De Wette, Wilhelm M. L. 1780–1849 German, OT and NT; identified the Deuteronomic Code as the book found in the Temple.

Dibelius, Martin 1883–1947 German, NT; pioneer form critic.

Dillmann, Christian F. A. 1823–94 German; Ethiopic studies.

Dodd, Charles H. 1884–1973 English, NT; realized eschatology.

Driver, Samuel R. 1846–1914 English Hebraist.

Duhm, Bernhard 1847–1924 German; separated 2nd and 3rd Isaiah.

Ebeling, Gerhard 1912– German; the New Hermeneutic.

Eichhorn, Johann G. 1752–1827 German; first major source critic of the Pentateuch.

Eichrodt, Walther 1890–1978 German; OT covenant theology.

Eissfeldt, Otto 1880–1973 German; OT source criticism.

Erasmus c. 1466–1536 From Rotterdam; edition of the Greek NT.

Fuchs, Ernst 1903– German; the New Hermeneutic.

Gesenius, Heinrich F. W. 1786–1842 German; OT lexicographer.

Graf, Karl H. 1815–69 German, OT; his work on 'P' formed the basis of the Graf–Wellhausen hypothesis.

Griesbach, Johann J. 1745–1812 German; pioneer NT text critic and the first to compile a synopsis.

Gunkel, Hermann 1862–1932 German, mainly OT; founder of form criticism.

Harnack, Adolf 1851–1930 German; early church historian.

Harris, J. Rendel 1852–1941 English; early Christian texts.

31

Hastings, James 1852–1922 Scottish; *Dictionary of the Bible* etc.

Heidegger, Martin 1889–1976 German; existentialist philosopher and the major influence on demythologization.

Holtzmann, Heinrich J. 1832–1910 German, NT; established the two-source hypothesis.

Hort, Fenton J. A. 1828–92 English; Wescott–Hort edition of the Greek NT.

Huck, Albert 1867–1942 German; synopsis.

Jeremias, Joachim 1900–79 German; sayings and parables of Jesus.

Jülicher, Adolf 1857–1938 German; major study on the parables.

Kähler, Martin 1835–1912 German, NT; proto-existentialist.

Käsemann, Ernst 1906– German, NT; Sätze heiligen Rechtes.

Kierkegaard, Søren A. 1813–55 Danish; major influence on existentialism.

Kittel, Gerhard 1888–1948 German; *Theological Dictionary of the NT*; son of Rudolf Kittel.

Kittel, Rudolf 1853–1929 German; *Biblia Hebraica*.

Kümmel, Werner G. 1905– German; the development of the NT.

Küng, Hans 1928– German Swiss theologian; *On Being a Christian*.

Lachmann, Karl 1793–1851 German, NT; founder of modern textual criticism.

Lagrange, Marie-Joseph 1855–1938 French; gospel commentaries.

Lessing, Gotthold E. 1729–81 German; proposed an Urevangelium.

Lightfoot, Robert H. 1883–1953 English; early form critic.

Loisy, Alfred 1857–1940 French; the leading Modernist.

Luther, Martin 1483–1546 German; the leading Reformation theologian.

Metzger, Bruce M. 1914– American; NT Greek text.

Migne, Jacques P. 1800–75 French; comprehensive editions of the Latin and Greek Fathers.

Montefiore, Claude J. G. 1858–1938 English; Jewish approach to the gospels.
Moule, Charles F. D. 1908– English; *The Phenomenon of the NT.*
Mowinckel, Sigmund O. P. 1884–1965 Norwegian; major study of the Psalms.
Nestle, Eberhard 1851–1913 German; major critical edition of the Greek NT.
Noth, Martin 1902–68 German; work on the amphictyony and the Deuteronomic History.
Nygren, Anders 1890–1978 Swedish theologian; *Agape and Eros.*
Otto, Rudolf 1869–1937 German; Jesus as the Suffering Servant.
Rahner, Karl 1904– German Jesuit; systematic theologian.
Reimarus, Hermann S. 1694–1768 German deist; earliest researcher into the life of Jesus.
Renan, Joseph E 1823–92 French; liberal 'Life of Jesus'.
Ritschl, Albrecht 1822–89 German; community basis of the Gospel.
Robinson, H. Wheeler 1872–1945 English; popular OT historian.
Robinson, James M. 1924– American, NT; *New Quest for the Historical Jesus.*
Robinson, John A. T. 1919– In Cambridge; early dating of the NT books; *Honest to God.*
Schillebeeckx, Edward C. F. 1914– Dutch Dominican; *Jesus.*
Schleiermacher, Friedrich E. D. 1768–1834 German; seminal literary critic of the NT.
Schweitzer, Albert 1875–1965 German; eschatological character of Jesus's preaching.
Schweizer, Eduard 1913– German Swiss; NT Church.
Stendahl, Krister 1921– Swedish American; NT hermeneutics.
Strauss, David F. 1808–74 German; radical life of Jesus.
Streeter, Burnett H. 1874–1937 English; Proto-Luke, 'L', 'M'.

Tillich, Paul 1886–1965 German; systematic theologian.

Tischendorf, Constantin 1815–74 German; discoverer of Bible manuscripts.

Von Rad, Gerhard 1901–71 German; *OT Theology*.

Weiss, Johannes 1863–1914 German; eschatological character of Jesus's mission.

Wellhausen, Julius 1844–1918 German; Graf–Wellhausen hypothesis on the development of the Pentateuch.

Westcott, Brooke F. 1825–1901 English bishop; Westcott–Hort edition of the Greek NT.

Wrede, William 1859–1906 German; messianic secret in Mark.

Modern English Bibles

Unless otherwise stated, the dates given are for the complete edition. The New Testament is often published separately some years before. Sometimes, indeed, the Old Testament is never finished. It must be dispiriting ten years or more after the beginning of the project to be faced with translating the two books of Chronicles, knowing that scarcely one per cent of those who buy the completed edition will ever read them. Perhaps it is as well that some give up: consider the number of trees cut down to supply the paper for those obscure, neglected pages.

Very few of these translations are in fact used in serious study. The safest and most widely accepted is the RSV. However, the study edition of the JB remains unrivalled for presentation.

Amplified Version 1958 American expansion of the ASV, aimed at bringing out the different shades of meaning in the text.

ASV – American Standard Version 1901 Revision of the RV by the American members of the committee.

AV – Authorized Version 1611

CB – Common Bible 1973 An edition of the RSV so arranged that it contains all the books in the canons of the Protestant, Roman Catholic and Orthodox Churches.

Douai–Rheims Bible 1609 English Roman Catholic translation of the Vulgate.

ERV – English Revised Version American name for the RV when contrasted with the ASV.

GNB – Good News Bible Another name for the TEV.

IB – Interpreter's Bible 1957 Not a translation, but a twelve volume set containing the AV and RSV in parallel columns with extensive notes and commentary.

JB – Jerusalem Bible 1955 First truly modern translation, in French, by the Dominicans of the Ecole Biblique in Jerusalem. English version 1966.

KJV – King James Version American name for the AV.

Knox Version 1955 Translation of the Vulgate by the Roman Catholic, Ronald Knox.

LB – Living Bible 1971 Conservative, Protestant paraphrase by the American, Kenneth Taylor.

Moffatt Version 1924 Colloquial translation in the AV tradition by the Scottish scholar, James Moffatt.

NAB – New American Bible 1970 Roman Catholic translation from the original texts.

NASB – New American Standard Bible 1963 A revision of the ASV.

NEB – New English Bible 1970 First major English translation, as opposed to a revision, since 1611.

NIV – New International Version 1978 Popular, readable translation by American Evangelicals.

NJV – New Jewish Version First edition of the Torah in 1962, and continuing through the rest of the Hebrew canon. An American translation, based on the Massoretic Text.

NKJV – New King James Version 1979 A curiosity of modern, American fundamentalism; by modernizing the AV alone, it avoids all the text critical conclusions of the last 300 years.

Phillips Version 1958 Translation of the New Testament by the Anglican parish priest, J. B. Phillips.

RSV – Revised Standard Version 1952 Comprehensive American revision of the ASV, in the AV tradition. Roman Catholic edition 1966.

RV – Revised Version 1885 Very literal, scholarly revision of the AV.

TEV – Today's English Version 1976 Simple, readable translation by the American Bible Society. English edition the same year.

TT – Translation for Translators New Testament in 1966; Old Testament incomplete. With notes added to bring out difficulties in the Greek and points of textual criticism, for those with only a partial grasp of the original.

WV – Westminster Version New Testament in 1935; Old Testament unfinished. Roman Catholic translation.

Glossary

Dates AD *unless specified. Small capitals indicate a cross-reference.*

Abba (Aramaic) 'Father!'; Mk. 14.36.

Abdias Latin form of OBADIAH.

Abgar Legend Apocryphal story, written in Syriac *c.* 300, recounting the exchange of letters between Abgar V, king of Edessa, and Christ. In a late addition to the legend, Jesus sends a portrait of himself miraculously imprinted on cloth (the Turin Shroud?).

abiogenesis Ancient belief that life can spring from dead matter; e.g. Samson and the bees that came from the carcass of the dead lion, Jg. 14.8.

ab ovo (Latin) 'From the egg'; from the *very* beginning.

Abraham, Apocalypse of Christian reworking of a Jewish apocryphon, recounting the conversion of Abraham from idolatry and his subsequent apocalyptic visions; written after AD 70, it argues that the destruction of Jerusalem was punishment for a false cult.

Abraham, Testament of Jewish, or perhaps Christian, apocryphon of possibly the 2nd cent. AD, relating Abraham's reluctant preparation for death, in which he meets the archangel Michael and Death himself. It urges a sympathetic concern for sinners and contains a vision of the two roads, leading to heaven and hell.

acatalectic (Hebrew poetry) Not CATALECTIC: complete in its syllables.

Accadian See AKKADIAN.

accommodation Adaptation of a text's meaning to fit altered circumstances; e.g. Hos. 11.1, 'I called my son out of Egypt', quoted at Mt. 2.15, referring to Jesus.

37

acolyte By extension, any attendant on the priest at a religious ceremony.

acrophony Use of the pictograph of an object to represent the initial sound, or syllable, of the name of that object; e.g. *aleph*, an ox, to represent *a*. One way of developing an alphabet.

acrostic (Hebrew poetry) Literary style in which the verses of a poem begin with the consecutive letters of the alphabet; the greatest example is Ps. 119.

actant One of the formal categories applied by structural analysis to a story. Part of an invariable system of classification called an *actantial model*, there are generally six actants (not the same as the actors of the narrative itself), Sender–Object–Receiver, Helper–Subject–Opponent.

Acts (Or, more fully, the *Acts of the Apostles*) The second part of Luke's narrative addressed to Theophilus, the first section dealing with the early years of the Church in Jerusalem, the second with Paul's missionary journeys. The WESTERN TEXT has a markedly longer recension.

Adam, Apocalypse of Coptic revelation from Nag Hammadi, with an original Greek text of the 1st or 2nd cent. AD, outlining 'the hidden gnosis of Adam which he gave to Seth'. Based on midrashic legends from Genesis, it gives a fully developed account of a Gnostic redeemer-myth that is Jewish and not Christian in origin.

Adam and Eve, Book of Jewish apocryphon, written between 20 BC and AD 70, and reworked by a Christian. Found in two recensions, a Latin *Vita Adae et Evae* and a shorter and older Greek text misnamed the *Apocalypse of Moses*; it records the last testaments and death of Adam and Eve, expounding the punishment of death and the promise of salvation.

Addai, Doctrine of Syriac work of *c.* 400, enlarging the older core of the ABGAR LEGEND and recounting the missionary visit to Edessa of Addai (Thaddaeus?).

ad hominem (Latin) Relating to an argument directed to the principles of the individual rather than of abstract truth.

adiaphora (Greek) 'Things indifferent'; matters not essential to faith, and so neither required nor forbidden.

ad loc. (Latin) At the passage already cited.

Adonai (Hebrew) 'Lord'. The substitute, the QERĒ PER-PETUUM, for the unpronounceably holy name of God, YHWH. (Greek: KYRIOS)

adoptionism Heretical belief that Jesus did not come into this world as the true Son of God, but merely became so by adoption, usually at his baptism.

aeon Gnostic term for the personification of an age, or later by extension a sphere of the heavens.

aetiology Study and explanation of causes. An aetiology is an explanation of the cause or origin of some particular tradition or phenomenon; they are especially prevalent in the early part of the OT, e.g. God's curse of the serpent, 'upon your belly shall you go', Gen. 3.14, may be based on an ancient aetiology of why snakes crawl rather than walk; Lot's wife being turned into a pillar of salt, Gen. 19.26, is an aetiology of a striking local feature.

affusion Pouring water over the head in baptism, as opposed to immersion or mere ASPERSION.

a fortiori (Latin) With stronger reason.

agape The Greek word for 'love' most often used in the NT; the word employed for 'love' in the context of the Christian Gospel, as opposed to two other Greek words, *eros* (passionate love) and *philia* (brotherly love).

If also refers to the 'love feast', a communal meal of the early Church related to but distinct from the Eucharist.

Aggadah See HAGGADAH.

Aggaeus Latin form of HAGGAI.

agglutination Characteristic of ancient and Semitic languages whereby words are built up from simple root forms without altering them.

agrapha (Greek) 'Unwritten'. Title given to sayings attributed to Jesus but not found in the canonical gospels, which have some claim to be considered genuine; either elsewhere in the NT, such as Acts 20.35, in the writings of the Fathers or in some apocryphal works, such as the Gospel of THOMAS.

Ahikar, Widsom of Folk tale, with long passages of Wisdom teaching, about Ahikar, Grand Vizier of Sennacherib, and his worthless, adopted son Nadan. Written in Mesopotamia, in Aramaic, 5th cent. BC or even earlier, it was widely known and had considerable influence, in particular on Tobit.

Akhmimic COPTIC dialect spoken in Upper Egypt; texts date from the 3rd to the 5th cent.

Akkadian The earliest Semitic language, it superseded Sumerian in Mesopotamia from the 3rd millenium; written in cuneiform, it spread to become the major international language of the ancient Near East, only replaced by Aramaic *c*. 500 BC. From the 2nd millenium, it is found in two main dialects, BABYLONIAN, the more important, and ASSYRIAN.

Aktionsart (German) 'Kind of action'. Term used to indicate a characteristic of Greek verbs in which the tenses distinguish more between the kind of action than between the time of that action; e.g. very roughly the aorist points to a momentary (punctiliar) action, 'he went', the imperfect to an extended (linear) action, 'he was going'.

Alalakh Texts 466 Akkadian texts giving details about the life, literature and religion of the city of Alalakh, near Antioch, between the 17th and 15th centuries BC.

Alexandrian Text An early and important form of the Greek NT, probably from Egypt, and found in Codices Vaticanus and Sinaiticus; formerly called the *Neutral Text.*

allography The use of a foreign ideograph or logogram for one of one's own words.

Alpha Recent designation for the text-type represented by A (Codex Alexandrinus), i.e. the LUCIANIC TEXT.

alterity The state of being other or different; a category in structural analysis.

amanuensis Someone who writes out, usually a letter, by dictation; e.g. Tertius for Paul, Rom. 16.22.

Amarna Tablets Diplomatic letters of the first half of the 14th cent. BC, from Tell el-Amarna in Egypt. Written in cuneiform Babylonian, they reflect the Egyptians' loss of control in Western Asia under Pharaohs Amen-hotep III and IV.

Amen-em-ope, Wisdom of Collection of Egyptian proverbs in thirty sections, written about the 10th cent. BC, with many close parallels to the SAYINGS OF THE WISE section of Proverbs.

'am ha'aretz (Hebrew) 'The people of the land'. In preexilic Judah, probably the provincial landowning class;

after the exile, for those who had remained in the region around Jerusalem; in rabbinic literature, a term of contempt for the ignorant.

Amidah (Hebrew) 'Standing'. Main series or service of prayers for daily use by Jews; it is based on the EIGHTEEN BENEDICTIONS.

a minore ad maius (Latin) 'From the lesser to the greater'; the equivalent of the Hebrew QAL WAHOMER.

Ammonian Sections Divisions marked in the margins of ancient manuscripts of the Gospels, to indicate parallel passages. Used as the basis for the EUSEBIAN CANONS, they may have been devised by Eusebius himself.

Amoraim Jewish scholars, the successors of the TANNAIM, who were active from the completion of the Mishnah, *c*.200, until the completion of the Talmud, *c*. 500, who compiled the GEMARA.

Amorite One of the early north-western Semitic languages, it is close to CANAANITE and with probable influence on the development of HEBREW.

Amos (Am.) The first of the written prophets, a shepherd from Judah who prophesied in the Northern Kingdom during the prosperous reign of Jeroboam II (786–746 BC). Chs. 1–2, oracles against the nations; 3–6, condemnation of Israel's gross sin and injustice; 7–9, visions of her approaching destruction.

amphictyony Confederation of neighbouring states or tribes, primarily for the sake of self-defence, based upon a common, shared shrine; as in pre-monarchical Israel, though the precise details are much disputed.

anabasis (Greek) 'Ascension'.

anacephalaiosis Greek for RECAPITULATION.

anacoluthon or **anacoluthia** The change to a new grammatical construction before the original one has been completed. Paul had this problem, e.g. Gal. 2.4–6 (twice).

anacrusis (Hebrew poetry) Added syllable or word at the beginning of a line of verse, often a term of address such as 'O Lord' inserted without concern for the parallelism.

anadiplosis (Hebrew poetry) Reduplication, where the second line of a couplet begins with the last or most prominent word of the first; e.g. Ps. 29.1, 'Pay tribute to the

Lord, O sons of God: tribute to the Lord of glory and power.'

Anaginoskomena   Greek equivalent of the Apocrypha/ Deuterocanonical Books.

anagogic interpretation   One that brings out the spiritual or mystical truth of the biblical text, that clarifies the eternal truth expressed in it.

analogue   Earthly analogy of something divine; e.g. fatherhood.

anamnesis   (Greek) 'Memorial', 'remembrance', referring to Christ's command at the Last Supper, 'Do this in remembrance of me', I Cor. 11.24. (Hebrew equivalent ZIKKARON)

anapaest   (Hebrew poetry) Verse metre that has one stressed (long) syllable at the end of each foot. Preceded by two unstressed syllables, it is the reverse of a DACTYL.

anaphora (1)   In literary analysis, the repetition of an opening word or phrase; e.g. 'By faith. . . .', Heb. 11.

(2)   In the liturgy, the central prayer of the Eucharist.

anastasis   (Greek) 'Resurrection'.

'anawim   (Hebrew) The 'poor', the 'humble'.

Andrew, Acts of   Though one of the earlier apocryphal Acts, quite long and influential, very little of it now remains; it consisted of a journey narrative and the *Martyrdom of Andrew*; Greek, late 2nd cent.

androgynous   Relating to the uniting of the sexual characteristics of male and female, and thus the removal of sexuality: a goal of many 2nd cent. Gnostics and Christian ascetics.

ANE   Common abbreviation for 'the ancient Near East', 'ancient' in this case ending *about* 500 BC.

angelolatry   Worship of angels.

angelology   That part of theology dealing with angels and their part in the divine economy.

angelophany   Visible manifestation of an angel; e.g. Gabriel to Mary, at the Annunciation, Lk. 1.26ff.

angelus interpres   Helpful heavenly being who interprets visions to those who have them, a characteristic of APOCALYPTIC literature; e.g. Gabriel to Daniel, 8.16ff.

aniconic   Relating to idols etc. that are not made in human or animal form.

anima mundi (Latin) 'Soul of the world'; the source of life.

animism Primitive belief that material objects such as stones and trees are possessed of a living spirit.

Ankündigung (German) '(Prophetic) announcement'.

anno mundi (Latin) 'In the year of the world'. The calculation of the Jewish calendar, dating from the creation of the world, fixed at 3761 BC.

antediluvian Before the Flood.

anthropomorphism Ascription of human form or attributes to God; making God in man's own image.

anthropopathy Ascription of human feelings and passions to God.

antilegomena Name given by Eusebius to those books that had a disputed claim to be part of the NT canon.

Anti-Marcionite Prologues Short introductions to the gospels, originally written in Greek in the 2nd cent. or perhaps later, and found in some manuscripts of the Vulgate.

antinomianism Belief that Christians, under the law of grace, are no longer bound by the moral laws. Often used pejoratively.

Antiochene Text Another name for the LUCIANIC TEXT.

antiphrasis The sarcastic use of a word to mean its opposite; e.g. Paul's use of the word 'wise' when writing to the Corinthians.

Anti-Royalist Source See ROYALIST SOURCE.

antistasis The dramatic repetition of a word but with a different meaning; e.g. I Cor. 1.21, 'As God in his wisdom ordained, the world would not find him by its wisdom'.

apatheia (Greek) 'Impassibility', 'freedom from emotion'.

Apiru See HABIRU.

Apocalypse, Little Modern title given to Mk. 13. In the OT, the same title is sometimes given to the ISAIAH APOCALYPSE.

Apocalypse, The Unless otherwise qualified, another name for REVELATION.

Apocalypse of Weeks See I ENOCH.

apocalyptic A genre of literature, and by extension a whole realm of thought, at its height between 200 BC and AD 100, that dealt with hidden revelations concerning the end of the present world order and the dawn of a new age of prosperity and the restoration of Israel. The two great examples are Daniel and Revelation.

It set out to answer the despair expressed in Ps. 74.9, 'There is no longer any prophet among us: there is no one who can tell us how long,' by assuring the faithful few, the true Israel, that the whole mechanism of world history was coming to an end and that God was indeed acting, for very soon all would be utterly changed and the full, glorious promise of salvation would be brought to fulfilment. Perhaps the most striking characteristic of the literature, beyond its vivid imagination of the mighty events to come, is a strongly determinist view of history coupled with an intense moral seriousness.

apocatastasis (Greek) 'Restoration'. Doctrine that in the end all men will be saved; also known as UNIVERSALISM.

Apocrypha Collection of books found in the Greek version of the OT, and therefore accepted as sacred by hellenistic Jews and the early Church, but not included in the Hebrew canon. Virtually the same as the DEUTEROCANONICAL BOOKS.

apocryphal The adjective is not generally applied to a book of the APOCRYPHA itself, but to an APOCRYPHON.

apocryphal Acts Genre of popular Christian literature developed from the model of the canonical Acts of the Apostles. They sought to supplement the NT material with legends and preaching, either to enhance the Apostle's reputation or for, usually gnostic or encratite, propaganda. Their most important characteristics are the journey motif and a martyrdom at the end, ARETALOGY and TERATOLOGY, erotic interest hidden under ascetic teaching and a strong element of preaching.

Those of the 2nd and 3rd cent., of JOHN, PETER, PAUL, ANDREW and THOMAS are of importance. There are others but they are all much later and heavily derivative with no significant theological intent.

apocryphon An anonymous or pseudonymous religious work, either Jewish or Christian, with implicit or explicit claim to divine inspiration, not from the APOCRYPHA but one entirely outside the canon, and generally falling within the period from the 2nd cent. BC to the 5th cent. AD.

apodeictic law   Absolute and universally applicable form of law, the classic types being 'Thou shalt not. . . .' and 'Whoever . . . shall be put to death'. In the early OT, it is the stern and uncompromising form of law that most clearly expresses the divine commands, and probably originated among nomadic tribes, as opposed to the secular and sedentary CASUISTIC LAW.

apodosis   The main clause of a conditional sentence, the 'if . . .' clause being the PROTASIS.

apologist   One who writes *apologetic*, or an *apologia*, the reasoned defence of one's faith, designed to persuade pagans of its truth; particularly applied to 2nd cent. Christian writers such as Justin Martyr, Aristides and Athenagoras.

apophatic theology   Approach that deliberately passes over in silence the object of central importance, the inexpressible nature and character of God. Sometimes called the *via negativa*.

apophthegm   (Plural: *apophthegmata*) A short, pithy saying, encapsulating an important truth. Used in a technical sense to refer to a short saying of Jesus set in a brief narrative context, what other scholars call a PARADIGM.

aporia   (Greek) 'Perplexity', 'impassibility'. Situation of no progress where a particular problem is so formulated that any solution only creates a further problem to be resolved.

aposiopesis   In speech or writing, a sudden cutting short.

apostasy   Renunciation of one's faith.

a posteriori   (Latin) 'That which follows' or is known by experience.

Apostolic Age   First period of the Christian Church, within the lifetime of the Apostles; AD 33+.

Apostolic Church Order   Christian manual of church order and moral discipline, written in Egypt *c.* 300, in Greek.

Apostolic Constitutions   Collection of church laws, based on the DIDACHE and DIDASCALIA, and containing in its last chapter the *Apostolic Canons*; written in Syria, late 4th cent.

Apostolic Fathers   Title given to the Christian writers of the period immediately after the *Apostolic Age*, after the NT was written: CLEMENT of Rome, IGNATIUS of Antioch, POLYCARP, HERMAS, PAPIAS, and the authors of the Epistle of BARNABAS, the Epistle to DIOGNETUS, II CLEMENT and the DIDACHE.

Apostolic Tradition Treatise on Christian rites and liturgy, written by Hippolytus of Rome in the early 3rd cent.

Apostolikon (Greek) 'Relating to an Apostle'. Generally of a passage or quotation from the Epistles, or sometimes the Gospels; in particular of Marcion's edited canon of Pauline Epistles, made c. 140.

apothegm See APOPHTHEGM.

apotheosis Pagan custom of deifying emperors and other great men after their death.

apotropaic Having the power to ward off evil influence; e.g. the blood upon the doorposts at the time of the Passover, Ex. 12.22f.

apparatus criticus Latin for CRITICAL APPARATUS.

a priori (Latin) 'That which precedes'; prior to or independent of experience.

apud (Latin) According to; in the writings of.

Aqhat, Legend of Incomplete Ugaritic myth from RAS SHAMRA, that appears to relate the death and resurrection of Aqhat, son of Dan'el.

Aquila, Version of Extremely literal translation of the Hebrew OT into Greek, made c. 130 AD by Aquila, a proselyte from Christianity to Judaism.

Aramaic Semitic language as old as and close to Hebrew. Found on inscriptions of the 9th cent. BC, it became from the 8th cent. increasingly important as a lingua franca of the ancient Near East; known as *Official Aramaic*, it gradually replaced AKKADIAN, reaching its height under the Neo-Babylonians and Persians until succeeded by Greek, c. 300 BC. Although there continued a form of *Standard Literary Aramaic* as a sort of secondary lingua franca, it also split into *Western* and *Eastern* dialects. The former included the Galilean dialect spoken by Jesus and his disciples, the latter SYRIAC.

archisynagogos (Greek) 'Head of the synagogue'. Leader whose main concern was the physical arrangements for synagogue worship.

archon Gnostic term for a subordinate ruler of an AEON or one of the spheres of the heavens.

aretalogy Hellenistic literary genre that recounts the marvellous and miraculous deeds of the hero, a god or one like a god, revelling in the description of his exceptional powers

46

and virtues. The most well-known example is Philostratus's 'Life of Apollonius of Tyana', which may have influenced the later Christian APOCRYPHAL ACTS. Not to be confused with ARETOLOGY.

aretology   That part of ethics that deals with virtue.

argumentum e silentio   (Latin) 'Argument from silence'; e.g. to argue that because a writer does not mention a particular event or subject, he is ignorant of it.

Aristeas, Letter of   Fictional account of the Septuagint translation of the Torah, commending Jewish learning in a world of Greek culture; c. 100 BC in Alexandria.

Ark Narrative   I Sam. 4–6, II Sam. 6. Description of the capture of the Ark from Shiloh by the Philistines, its return and its later move to Jerusalem.

Ascents, Songs of   Another name for the PILGRIMAGE SONGS.

asherah   (Hebrew) Sacred tree or pole of Canaanite fertility worship, connected with the goddess of the same name.

askesis   (Greek) 'Training'; spiritual self-discipline.

aspersion   Baptism by merely sprinkling the water over the head.

assimilation   Scribal error, whether deliberate or unintentional, of replacing the wording in the text by a reading from another similar book; particularly common in the Synoptic Gospels, e.g. Luke's version of the Lord's Prayer, 11.2ff.

associative relations   Occasional synonym for PARADIGMATIC RELATIONS.

assonance   (Hebrew poetry) Recurrence of the same or similar vowel sounds in the accented syllables of a distich or longer unit of verse.

Assyrian   Semitic, cuneiform language; with BABYLONIAN one of the two main dialects of AKKADIAN.

asyndeton   Literary style in which two consecutive phrases are not connected by a conjunction where one would normally expect one; a characteristic of Mark's Gospel.

athetize   Reject a text or passage as spurious.

Aton, Hymn to   Monotheistic praise of Aton the sun god, lord of all creation, from the time of Pharaoh Akhenaton (Amenhotep IV), 1364–1347 BC; it has some striking parallels with Ps. 104.

atonement The reconciliation (at-one-ment) of man with God.

Atrahasis Old Babylonian text on three clay tablets, *c.* 1700 BC but based on earlier Sumerian sources, that describes the creation of men from earth and blood, the sending of a flood to destroy them, and the saving of Atrahasis with his family and animals in the ark he had built.

autograph The original manuscript of a book of the Bible in the author's own handwriting; none remain.

autonomy Ethical assertion that the moral laws are, and ought to be, self-imposed; the opposite view is HETERONOMY.

autosoterism Doctrine that man can save himself by his own efforts.

axiology That part of philosophy that deals with the nature of value and values.

Azariah, Prayer of First part of the Song of the THREE CHILDREN.

Baal and Anath One of the RAS SHAMRA TEXTS, being a legend of the rain-god Baal and the warrior-goddess Anath, that gives us an excellent picture of Ugaritic mythology.

Babylonian Semitic, cuneiform language; more important than ASSYRIAN the other main dialect of AKKADIAN. *Old Babylonian* is found in the Code of Hammurabi, *c.* 1700 BC; *Middle Babylonian* in the Amarna archives, 14th cent. BC; *Neo-Babylonian* in the writings of the Babylonian Empire, 7th cent. BC; *Late Babylonian* in the Persian period.

Babylonian Chronicle Contemporary historical archives that cover most of the years of the Neo-Babylonian Empire (626–539 BC), recording such events as the capture of Nineveh and of Jerusalem. The last part is usually called the NABONIDUS CHRONICLE.

bamah (Hebrew) 'High place'. Canaanite form of local shrine and place of sacrifice, taken over by Israelites but later suppressed.

bar– (Aramaic) 'Son (of)'.

Baraithah A Rabbinic text of the first two Christian centuries not included in the Mishnah; often, more precisely, those texts neither in the MISHNAH nor TOSEPHTA, but which are cited in the Jerusalem and Babylonian Talmuds.

Barnabas, Epistle of Christian treatise, counted among the APOSTOLIC FATHERS, against the Mosaic law and worship and a literal interpretation of the OT. It also includes a version of the DUAE VIAE parallel to that in the Didache; written in Greek, at Alexandria, between AD 70 and 100.

Bar Nasha (Aramaic) 'Son of Man'; Dan. 7.13.

Baruch, Books of Four works by different authors that have been ascribed to Baruch, the scribe of Jeremiah:

I (in the Apocrypha) Written in Hebrew, now lost, and edited between 150 and 50 BC, it consists of two, perhaps originally separate, parts: 1.1–3.8, a prose introduction and prayer of confession, and 3.9–5.9, two poems, one in praise of God's wisdom, the other of comfort and restoration. The Letter of JEREMIAH is sometimes included as ch. 6.

II Syriac Apocalypse of Baruch Like IV EZRA, a series of revelations from the time of the fall of Jerusalem in 587 BC to encourage those who had experienced the fall of AD 70; Hebrew, late 1st cent. AD.

III Greek Apocalypse of Baruch Visions of the seven heavens, from the 2nd cent. AD; a Jewish text reworked by a Christian.

IV Rest of the Words of Baruch Jewish-Christian work about the end of Jeremiah's life; 2nd cent. AD.

Bashmuric Earlier and misleading name for the FAYYUMIC dialect of Coptic.

basileia (Greek) 'Kingdom', 'reign'.

bath qol (Hebrew) 'Daughter of a voice'. Rabbinic term for a voice from heaven. With the cessation of prophecy it remained the only means of communication from God to man.

BCE Abbreviation for Before the Common Era, and thus the non-Christian equivalent for the years BC.

Bearbeiter (German) 'Compiler', 'reviser'; one who works over the sources: an early redactor.

beatific vision The full vision of God in his glory; e.g. Paul's experience, II Cor. 12.2ff.

Beatitudes Mt. 5.3–11 and Lk. 6.20–2.

Begriffsgeschichte (German) 'History of concepts'.

Beispielerzählungen (German) 'Example stories', such as the Story of the Good Samaritan, more developed than the classic parable.

Bel and the Dragon One of the later additions to Daniel, found as ch. 14 in the Septuagint and Vulgate or as a separate book of the Apocrypha. Written in the 1st or 2nd cent. BC, probably in Greek, it consists of two popular, polemical tales against idols and their priests.

ben– (Hebrew) 'Son (of)'.

Benedictus Lk. 1.68–79. The Song of Zechariah.

Ben Sira The author of SIRACH or *Ecclesiasticus*.

berakhah (Hebrew) 'Blessing'. The characteristic Jewish prayer of thanksgiving.

Bereshith Hebrew name for GENESIS.

berith (Hebrew) 'Covenant', in particular that between Yahweh and Israel.

Beta Recent designation for the text-type represented by B (Codex Vaticanus), i.e. the ALEXANDRIAN TEXT.

beth (Hebrew) 'House'. Compound of several names.

Bewährungschristologie (German) Doctrine that Jesus earned his exaltation to Son of God through his total virtue and obedience.

Biblical Antiquities Jewish apocryphon rewriting history from Adam to Saul, concentrating on the period of the Judges, urging strong leadership of the nation; probably late 1st cent. AD.

Biblical Theology Expression with a wide number of connotations; generally of an approach that seeks to build a complete theology from the Bible alone; more specifically for a trend at its height in the 1950s that gave careful study to the books, texts and especially words, on the hypothesis of a common, Hebraic viewpoint shared by all the biblical writers.

biblicism Adherence to the letter of the Bible to the exclusion of other authorities. Much the same, though more limited in scope, as FUNDAMENTALISM, it is less commonly used.

bibliolatry Pejorative term for an excessive veneration of the words of Scripture.

bicolon (Hebrew poetry) A couple of lines of verse complete in itself – a couplet; the basic form of OT verse. The term *distich* is perhaps more generally used.

Bildhälfte (German) 'Picture half'; the imagery of a parable as opposed to the meaning or teaching (SACHHÄLFTE).

binary opposition Simply, opposites. Structuralism's adherence to Cartesian logic demands a direct opposite for each major category of analysis; e.g. identity – non-identity, alterity – non-alterity.

Bodmer Papyri   Collection of important Greek and Coptic manuscripts, possibly from an Egyptian monastery, containing a wide range of Christian texts dating back to AD 200.

Bohairic   COPTIC dialect. Originally restricted to the western Delta area, it became in the later Christian centuries the principle literary language of the Church in Egypt.

bona fide   (Latin) 'In good faith'; with no deception.

boustrophedon   Characteristic of some ancient writing, in which the script goes in alternate lines from right to left and left to right.

brachy-catalectic   (Hebrew poetry) Line lacking a foot or two syllables.

brevior lectio potior   (Latin) In textual criticism, the shorter of two readings is to be preferred, as it is more likely to be original.

Byzantine Text   Standard form of the Greek NT text as used in Constantinople, the capital of the eastern Empire, and found in the great majority of extant manuscripts. Essentially the LUCIANIC TEXT, it became the basis for the TEXTUS RECEPTUS.

c. or **ca.**   (Latin: *circa*) 'About'; approximately.

Cabbalism   See KABBALAH.

Caesarean Text   One of the forms of the Greek text of the Gospels, reckoned to have been used at Caesarea in the 3rd cent.

caesura   (Hebrew poetry) Pause in the middle of the standard two-line verse.

Canaanite   One of the north-western Semitic group of languages, it is close to HEBREW and ARAMAIC. With relatively few texts, it tends to be a rather broad description, sometimes reckoned to include, rather than be distinct from, UGARITIC. Heiroglyphic, then cuneiform, then alphabetic.

canon   List of the books of the Bible accepted by the tradition and authority of the Rabbis or the Church as genuine and inspired and containing the rule of faith. Whence CANONICAL.

canonical   Belonging to or found in the Bible (the *canon*).

canonical criticism   Study of the biblical texts as we have them before us now and as they have been transmitted by the worshipping community of Jews or Christians. An approach that seeks to include and understand all the glosses, alterations and additions, as opposed to the various forms of HISTORICAL CRITICISM that tend to reject them as unimportant.

The classic example is *Amos*. The historical approach virtually ignored the epilogue, 9.11–15, as an unimaginative and inappropriate addition of the post-exilic editors. The canonical approach asks: How do these concluding words of restoration alter one's understanding of the preceding prophecies of doom? How do they make the message of an 8th cent. prophet relevant to a later generation? What does the work as a whole now mean to us as Scripture?

Canticle of Canticles   Rarer name for the Song of SOLOMON.

cantor   Soloist who leads liturgical singing.

Captivity Epistles   Ephesians, Philippians, Colossians, Philemon. Four letters traditionally believed to have been written by Paul while in prison in Rome.

caritas   (Latin) 'Charity', 'love'. (Greek: AGAPE)

casuistic law   Form of law that is applicable only in certain cases, its basic form being 'If . . ., then . . ..', to which further clauses can be added making its application yet more precise. The most widespread form of law in the ancient Near East, it is not essentially religious but appears characteristic of a settled, propertied society. In contrast to APODEICTIC LAW, which they brought from their nomadic, Yahwistic past, the early Hebrews most probably took it over from the Canaanites among whom they settled.

catachresis   Improper use of words.

catalectic   (Hebrew poetry) Line lacking a syllable in the last foot.

catechesis   (Greek) Instruction in the faith given before baptism to CATECHUMENS.

catechumens   Recent converts to Christianity, candidates for baptism.

catena   (Latin) 'Chain'. A series of quotations from the Church Fathers that make up a commentary upon a text of Scripture.

Catholic   Used in the context of early Christianity to refer to the orthodox, historically continuous, Church as against heretical, especially Gnostic, groups.

Catholic Epistles   James, I & II Peter, I (and sometimes II & III) John, Jude; so called because they are universal, and not addressed to specific people or churches.

catholicizing tendency   The tendency evident in later NT writings towards the institutionalizing of the Church and Christian belief; e.g. the ordering of bishops, I Tim. 3.1ff.

caveat   (Latin) 'Let him beware'. A caution or warning.

CE   Abbreviation for COMMON ERA.

cento   (Latin) 'Patchwork' of biblical quotations; e.g. Rom. 3.10ff.

cf.   (Latin: *confer*) 'Compare'.

ch./chs.   Chapter/chapters.

Chaldee   Misleading synonym for ARAMAIC, no longer used.

charismata   Greek plural of *charisma*, which is sometimes anglicized to *charism*, hence the occasional plural form *charisms*. The gifts given by the grace of God to every Christian for the fulfilment of his vocation, more especially the supernatural gifts such as healing and prophecy, I Cor. 12.4–11.

chesed   See HESED.

Chester Beatty Papyri   Collection of papyrus codices, probably from an Egyptian monastery and perhaps the same library as the BODMER PAPYRI; they provide valuable early evidence for the text of the Greek OT and NT.

chiasmus   Literary inversion. In its simplest form, A–B–B–A; e.g. Mk. 2.27, 'The Sabbath was made for man, not man for the Sabbath.' Also known as *chiastic*, or *inverted*, *parallelism*.

chiliasm   (From the Greek for a thousand) Essentially synonymous with MILLENARIANISM.

Chi-Rho   The first two letters, XP, of the Greek for *Christ*, an ancient abbreviation, or cryptogram, with the letters often superimposed.

chria   Brief narrative unit built around a striking saying (of Jesus) made to a particular person at a particular time; e.g. the three sayings on the seriousness of discipleship, Lk. 9.57ff.

Not all scholars would distinguish between this and a PRONOUNCEMENT STORY.

chrism The consecrated oil used in anointing at baptism and for healing etc.

Christology That part of theology that is concerned with the person of Christ, in particular the union of his human and divine natures.

Christophany Occasional term for Christ's post-resurrection appearances, to which one may add the Transfiguration and the confrontation with Paul on the way to Damascus.

Christ's Glory, Song of Phil. 2.6–11. Possibly an early hymn incorporated by Paul.

Chronicler Author of Chronicles, Ezra and Nehemiah.

Chronicles, I (I Ch.) Chs. 1–9, a series of genealogies; 10–29, an idealized account of David, the great monarch and true founder of the Temple worship. With II Chronicles, originally part of a single book, it forms a comprehensive rewriting of the history of the period of the monarchy, designed to enhance the importance of the Temple and its worship; mid-4th cent. BC.

Chronicles, II (II Ch.) Chs. 1–9, an idealized account of Solomon; 10–36, history of the Divided Kingdom down to the Exile.

circumlocution A roundabout expression; increasingly used from the 4th cent. BC onwards in relation to God, to avoid using his sacred name or any possible suggestion of anthropomorphism.

Clement, I Greek epistle by their bishop Clement sent by the Church at Rome to the Church at Corinth, in the last years of the 1st cent., after some of the younger men there had deposed their leaders. A major source of information on the establishment of the ministry in the Sub-Apostolic Age.

Clement, II Often counted among the APOSTOLIC FATHERS along with the first epistle, although almost certainly not by Clement of Rome, rather the earliest extant Christian sermon, from the mid-2nd cent., giving evidence of many non-canonical sayings of Jesus current at the time.

Clementine Epitomes Later paraphrases of the narrative in the *Homilies* and *Recognitions*, omitting the theological and philosophical reflections.

Clementine Homilies   Apocryphal narrative with accompanying preaching, philosophizing and legend, in Greek from Jewish-Christian circles in the 2nd cent., recounting Clement of Rome's journey to the east where he joins Peter in his contest with Simon Magus. Possibly dependent upon, and at very least closely connected with, the KERYGMATA PETROU.

Clementine Recognitions   Early 3rd cent. rewriting and expansion of the *Homilies*, of the same provenance, with added stories about Clement and his family, and in which the (secret) Jewish tradition of Peter and James is further emphasized.

codex   (Plural: *codices*) An ancient manuscript in book form, of vellum or papyrus. Used especially by Christians from at least as early as the 2nd cent., in contrast to the Jews who favoured the scroll.

Codex Alexandrinus   (A) Early 5th cent. Greek Bible, presented to King James I by the Patriarch of Constantinople; probably written in Egypt, it has the LUCIANIC TEXT for the Gospels, the ALEXANDRIAN for the rest of the NT.

Codex Bezae   (D) 5th cent. manuscript of the Gospels and Acts, now in Cambridge, with Greek and Latin texts on facing pages; it is the principal witness of the WESTERN TEXT.

Codex Ephraemi   (C) 5th cent. palimpsest remnant of the Greek Bible, with ALEXANDRIAN, WESTERN and BYZANTINE readings.

Codex Koridethi   (Θ) Primary witness to the CAESAREAN TEXT of Mark's Gospel; 9th cent.

Codex Sinaiticus   (ℵ, or sometimes S) Late 4th cent. Greek Bible, discovered in St. Catherine's Monastery on Mount Sinai; with B it is the chief witness to the ALEXANDRIAN TEXT.

Codex Vaticanus   (B) Early 4th cent. Greek Bible, probably written in Alexandria and now in the Vatican Museum; ALEXANDRIAN TEXT.

cognate   (Of words) From the same root, of the same family.

cohortative   Relating to exhortation. In Hebrew, the first person equivalent of the imperative, 'I will . . .'.

colometric   The writing of a text in which each line consists of one colon or clause.

colophon   Paragraph added at the end of a manuscript, giving details of the place and date of copying.

Colossians   (Col.) Either written by Paul when in prison in the early 60s or by a later deutero-pauline author; with many parallels with Ephesians, it is generally reckoned to have the better claim to pauline authorship.

Common Era   (CE) Non-Christian equivalent for the years *Anno Domini*.

Community Rule   (1QS, formerly DSD) (Also known as the *Manual of Discipline*) Hebrew text that has been built up and added to during the 2nd and early 1st cent. BC, outlining the organization, rules and discipline of the Qumran community.

comparative religion   Scientific and historical study of the world's religions and their mutual relations.

confessio fidei   (Latin) 'Confession of faith'.

confiteor   (Latin) 'I confess'. A confession of sins.

conflation   Copyist's compromise whereby two variant readings are combined to form a third.

Consolation, (Little) Book of   Occasional name for Jeremiah chs. 30 and 31, and sometimes chs. 32 and 33 as well.

Consolation of Israel, Book of the   Occasional name for DEUTERO-ISAIAH.

contra   (Latin) 'Against' the hypothesis of such-and-such a scholar.

controversy dialogue   Short narrative passage in the gospels containing a pronouncement of Jesus in reply to an attack by his critics; e.g. Mk. 12.13–17 on the question of paying tribute money to Caesar. Essentially therefore a sub-section of PRONOUNCEMENT STORIES. (German: *Streitgespräch*)

Coptic   Directly descended from ancient Egyptian, it was the language of Christian Egypt. No doubt spoken centuries before, it only became a literary language with the adoption of an alphabet, essentially Greek with a few additions, for the purposes of translating the Bible. Its two principal dialects were SAHIDIC and BOHAIRIC, with FAYYUMIC, AKHMIMIC and SUB-AKHMIMIC, to which may be added *Oxyrhynchite* from around Oxyrhynchus and *Dialect P* found in a 4th cent. papyrus codex, Bodmer 6.

Corinthians, I (I Cor.) Written by Paul, from Ephesus, AD 55?, to the Church which he had established some five years before.

Corinthians, II (II Cor.) Slightly later than the first epistle, chs. 10–13 could be part of an earlier letter to the church, making at least three in all.

Corinthians, III Apocryphal reply to an equally apocryphal letter from that church, anti-gnostic in character and forming part of the Acts of PAUL.

corporate personality Term, much used and much disputed, for the Hebrew conception of personal identity, that is markedly less individualistic than our own, but rather, tied up with the larger identity of the tribe or nation.

corpus (Latin) 'Body'. A complete or comprehensive body of writings.

Cosmocrater (Greek) 'Ruler of the world'. In Christian writing a title of the Devil; in Gnostic thought a lesser deity having part of the created order under his control.

cosmogony Theory of the creation of the universe.

cosmography Description or mapping of the universe.

cosmolatry Worship of the universe.

cosmology Study of the universe as a whole.

Court History Another name for the SUCCESSION NARRATIVE.

Covenant, Book of the or **Covenant Code** Ex. 20.22–23.33. Early collection of laws and regulations, both APODEICTIC and CASUISTIC, completed at least pre-650 BC, but with roots going back to the earliest days of settlement in Canaan.

creatio ex nihilo (Latin) Doctrine that the world was created from nothing. Gen. 1 appears to uphold this view, as against the earlier tradition of 2.5ff, where order and fertility are brought to a barren world of chaos.

Creation Epic, Akkadian See ENUMA ELISH.

creationism (1) (Sometimes when regarded as a contemporary phenomenon *Neo-Creationism*; or by its exponents *Scientific Creationism*.) Fundamentalist reaction to the evolutionary theory of Darwin and the whole approach of modern science, that asserts the absolute 'scientific' (and therefore verifiable) truth of the account of creation found in Gen. 1.

(2) Doctrine that God creates a brand new soul for each human being that is born. Contrary to TRADUCIANISM.

credo (Latin) 'I believe'. A creed, or confession of faith.

critical apparatus List of manuscript readings differing from the Greek or Hebrew text, placed at the bottom of the page in printed editions of the Bible.

crux interpretum (Latin) The nub of the problem.

cryptogram (Greek) 'Hidden writing'. A text or drawing with a secret meaning; e.g. the writing on the wall at Belshazzar's feast in Dan. 5.24ff, or the number 666 in Rev. 13.18.

cui bono (Latin) 'Who is benefited thereby?'

Cult-History School See KULTGESCHICHTLICHE SCHULE.

Cultic Decalogue Another name for the RITUAL DECA-LOGUE.

cult prophet One attached to a shrine or temple and having a liturgical function; they appear from about the rise of the monarchy to the fall of the Second Temple, but were never as significant as the independent prophets of the LORD.

cultural relativism The view that insists that the culture and thought patterns of say 1st cent. Palestine are so radically different to our own, that we cannot properly understand the ideas expressed in the literature that it produced; or again, that the Bible cannot mean the same thing to us as it did to those who wrote it.

cultus Latin for 'cult', no more than that.

cum grano salis (Latin) 'With a pinch of salt'.

cuneiform Wedge-shaped or arrow-headed characters used in many ancient, Near Eastern scripts; usually impressed with a stylus on clay tablets, but also carved in stone.

cursive script That which is written in small, joined letters – what we would regard as ordinary handwriting.

Cyrus Cylinder Written in cuneiform Babylonian on a small clay barrel in 536 BC, it records Cyrus's capture of Babylon guided by the god Marduk, and his policy of returning exiled peoples to their own countries.

D The DEUTERONOMIC source within the Pentateuch,

making up the bulk of the book of Deuteronomy (chs. 1–30). In the NT, D stands for Codex Bezae.

dabar   (Hebrew) 'Word'.

dactyl   (Hebrew poetry) Metre consisting of one stressed (long) syllable followed by two unstressed syllables; the reverse of an ANAPAEST.

daghesh   Dot placed in the middle of certain Hebrew letters to harden the sound at the beginning of a word, or to double it in the middle of a word.

dallat ha'aretz   (Hebrew) 'The poor of the land'.

Damascus Document   (CD) (Formerly called the *Zadokite Work*) Discovered in the Cairo Geniza and later at Qumran, it consists of the *Admonitions*, which reinterpret biblical prophecies to relate to the Essene community and includes the theme of the New Covenant in the land of Damascus, and the *Commandments*, which interpret and develop the Torah. In Hebrew, between 100 and 75 BC.

Daniel   (Dan.) The first and greatest work of APOCALYPTIC, made up of six WISDOM stories and four interpreted dream-visions, based on the shadowy figure of Daniel in the Babylonian period. Written during the persecution of Antiochus Epiphanes, 167–164 BC, to encourage fellow Jews to remain faithful, for God is about to act and a new age will dawn. 2.4b–7.28 is in Aramaic, the rest in Hebrew. For later additions to the book, see BEL AND THE DRAGON, SUSANNA AND THE ELDERS and the Song of the THREE CHILDREN.

daughter translation   Translation of the OT made not from the original Hebrew but from the Greek Septuagint.

Davidic Psalter, First   Pss. 3–41. One of the earliest, pre-exilic, collections of Psalms.

Davidic Psalter, Second   Pss. 51–72. Early collection of Psalms, probably from the same period as the First, included in the larger ELOHIST PSALTER.

Dead, Book of the   Modern title for a large collection of papyri from ancient Egypt, outlining magic and confessional formulae to protect the dead from evil powers. From the mid-2nd millenium BC onwards, they undoubtedly have a long tradition behind them.

Dead Sea Scrolls   Texts from the Jewish community at *Qumran* on the north-western edge of the Dead Sea, discovered in 1947, and written or copied between 200 BC and AD 70, in Hebrew and Aramaic, with some in Greek. They have provided a major new source of information on sectarian and apocalyptic Judaism of the 1st cent. AD, with all its possible influence on the early development of Christianity in Palestine, as well as some of the earliest manuscripts of the Hebrew Bible.

Debir (Hebrew) The innermost room of the Temple; the Holy of Holies.

Deborah, Song of Jg. 5. An ancient Hebrew victory song; possibly the oldest text of the OT, 12th cent. BC.

Decalogue The Ten Commandments, unless otherwise qualified: Ex. 20.1–17 and Deut. 5.6–22.

Decretum Gelasianum Latin list of books that were or were not to be regarded as Scripture; it reflects the Roman Church's view of the CANON in the early 6th cent.

de-eschatologizing tendency Apparent tendency in later NT writings to remove the element of ESCHATOLOGY in the teaching of Jesus, following the evident continuation of the present world and the delay of the expected PAROUSIA.

de facto (Latin) In reality; as a matter of fact.

Degrees, Songs of Another name for the PILGRIMAGE SONGS.

deism Belief in the existence of God, but not in a personal, involved God; particularly characteristic of the Enlightenment.

de jure (Latin) 'By right'; according to law.

Delta Recent designation for the text-type represented by D (Codex Bezae), i.e. the WESTERN TEXT.

demiurge From the Greek for 'craftsman', Gnostic term for the inferior deity, often identified with the god of the OT, who created the material world.

demotic script Simplified form, developed in the Persian period, of the Egyptian HIERATIC SCRIPT, itself a simplified form of HIEROGLYPHS.

demythologization (From the German *Entmythologisierung*, a technical term in the theology of R. Bultmann.) A reinterpretation of the biblical myths in EXISTENTIALIST terms; e.g. 'heaven' and 'hell' should not be seen as saying anything about cosmology, but rather as expressing truths about man and his relationship with God. The myths are not then eliminated, but understood in terms of man's existence rather than the structure of the universe. In this way the biblical truths can be made to cross the cultural and intellectual gap between the 1st cent. and the 20th.

Deo volente   (Latin) 'God willing'.

de profundis   First words in Latin of Ps. 130, used for a song of misery and repentance.

Descent into Hell   4th cent. Greek account of Christ among the imprisoned souls of Hades. With the Acts of PILATE it makes up the *Gospel of Nicodemus*.

Deus absconditus   (Latin) 'The hidden God'.

deuterocanonical books   Name for the books of the APOCRYPHA, minus I & II Esdras and the Prayer of Manasseh, included within the full canon of the OT in the Latin Bibles.

Deuterocanonical is also occasionally used of passages that have been shown by textual criticism to be secondary, e.g. Mk. 16.9–20.

deuterograph   A later rewriting of earlier material or a reappraisal of a subject; e.g. Chronicles is a deuterograph of Samuel and Kings, the Deuteronomic Code of the Book of the Covenant.

Deutero-Isaiah   Isaiah chs. 40–55; though sometimes, confusingly, the title is made to include 56–66, more properly called TRITO-ISAIAH. Written *c.* 540 BC, just before the fall of Babylon to the armies of Cyrus, to encourage the exiled people of Judah, it proclaims YHWH as Lord of all creation and promises a glorious restoration, a highway of salvation through the desert. It includes the figure of the SUFFERING SERVANT.

Deuteronomic/Deuteronomistic   Strictly, the former relates to the writers of Deuteronomy, the latter to the writers of the History and the collectors of the Prophets who follow their style and ideas. The ugliness of the second term and the fact that it is usually clear who is intended have led to the first frequently being used for both.

Deuteronomic Code   Deut. 12–26. Oldest, legal section of DEUTERONOMY, much of it a reworking of the Book of the COVENANT. It is generally equated with the 'Book of the Law' found in the Jerusalem Temple in 621 BC (II Kg. 22.8), and behind, or at least connected with, Josiah's religious reforms.

Deuteronomic History (DH) Deut. 1–4, Joshua, Judges, I & II Samuel, I & II Kings. Edited from earlier sources into a continuous history of Israel and Judah from the Conquest to the Exile, in the framework of obedience and blessing, disobedience and punishment; completed *c.* 550 BC, in Judah.

Deuteronomy (Deut.) Chs. 1–4, probable introduction to the DEUTERONOMIC HISTORY; 5–11, historical introduction to 12–26, the DEUTERONOMIC CODE; 27–30, additions to the Code; 31–4, conclusion to the Pentateuch, carrying on from the end of Numbers. Written in the form of speeches by Moses in the plain of Moab, just east of Canaan, it is the reinterpretation by the Deuteronomists for a later generation of the whole Sinai covenant.

Deutero-Pauline Letters Later works not by Paul himself but by someone following his style and ideas. In particular the PASTORAL EPISTLES.

Deutero-Zechariah Zechariah chs. 9–14. Two collections of PROTO-APOCALYPTIC oracles, 9–11 and 12–14 (sometimes called *Trito-Zechariah*), added *c.* 300 BC.

diachronic (Greek) 'Through time'. In relation to a language or a text, that which is concerned in any way with its evolution or historical development. As opposed to SYNCHRONIC.

diacritical signs Dots or other marks used to indicate different sounds of the same letter; e.g. the daghesh point in Hebrew.

Diaspora The Dispersion of the Jews – those living outside Palestine. From the 3rd cent. BC they increasingly spoke Greek rather than Hebrew or Aramaic, and by the 1st cent. AD greatly outnumbered the Jews in Palestine.

Diatessaron Harmony of the four Gospels by Tatian, a Syrian from Mesopotamia, *c.* 150; probably using the original Greek, he put together all their phrases into one continuous narrative; very little remains.

diatheke (Greek) 'Covenant', 'testament'.

Kaine Diatheke 'New Testament'.

diatribe In biblical, literary analysis, as opposed to common usage, an imaginary dialogue form used in moral teaching.

didache (Greek) 'Teaching'. The element of instruction

within the gospel message, as distinct from the generally prior proclamation or KERYGMA.

Didache, The Short, simple but very important early Christian manual on morals and church order. The first part contains the best example of the DUAE VIAE genre; the second instruction concerning baptism, fasting, the Eucharist, prophets, visiting apostles and so on. Written in two stages, *c.* 60, in Greek, possibly in Syria. It is probably the oldest Christian text outside the NT.

Didascalia Manual of church discipline, written in Syria, early in the 3rd cent. in Greek, expanding earlier sources such as the DIDACHE.

dies irae (Latin) 'The Day of Wrath'.

diglots Editions of the Bible with two texts or translations in parallel columns, in particular Graeco-Latin manuscripts from the 5th cent. onwards, such as Codex Bezae.

dikaiosune (Greek) 'Righteousness', 'uprightness'.

dimorphic Occurring in two distinct forms.

dimorphic society One (such as very early Israel?) where nomadic tribes and a sedentary population live together in mutual dependence.

Diognetus, Letter to Apologetic letter by an unknown Christian, noted for its description of Christians as the soul of the world, that is counted among the APOSTOLIC FATHERS; in Greek, 2nd cent.

diorthosis (Greek) The revision, recension, setting straight of a literary work.

disciplina arcani (Latin) 'Discipline of the secret'. The practice of concealing certain important rites and doctrines from all but full members of the Church. Often reckoned to explain John's omission from his gospel of Christ's baptism and the Last Supper.

Dispersion See DIASPORA.

distich (Hebrew poetry) A couple of lines of verse complete in itself—a couplet; the basic form of OT verse. The same as a *bicolon*.

dittography Unintentional repetition of letters or words by a copyist. Opposite error to HAPLOGRAPHY.

docetism Heretical doctrine, particularly widespread in the 2nd cent. AD and taken up into Gnosticism, which asserted that Christ's body, and therefore importantly his suffering on the cross, was only apparent and not real. The spiritual Christ was often seen as descending at the Baptism and ascending just before the Crucifixion.

Doctrina Apostolorum   Latin text of the 1st cent. AD that parallels the Duae Viae section of the DIDACHE.

documentary hypothesis   Essentially synonymous with the GRAF–WELLHAUSEN HYPOTHESIS.

dodecalogue   Set of twelve commandments or prohibitions; e.g. Deut. 27.15ff.

Dodekapropheton   (Greek)   The 'Twelve (minor) Prophets'.

dominical   Relating to the Lord Jesus Christ.

double tradition   Material common to both Matthew and Luke; the phrase is used to avoid any particular hypothesis, such as a shared dependence on a source document.

doxology   Formal praise of God found, usually at the end, in letters or the liturgy; e.g. Jude 24f, or the conclusion of the Lord's Prayer.

Dream Visions of Enoch   See I ENOCH.

Drohrede   (German) '(Prophetic) threat (of intervention by God)'.

DSS   Abbreviation for the DEAD SEA SCROLLS.

Duae Viae   (Latin) 'The Two Ways' of life and death, or of good and evil, derived from Moses' challenge to the people of Israel, 'I have set before you this day life and good, death and evil. . . . Choose life. . . .', Deut. 30.15–20. Important literary genre for moral teaching in late OT Judaism and early Christianity, the best example being in the DIDACHE. In the NT, note the broad and the narrow way of Mt. 7.13f.

dunamis   (Greek) 'Power' whether abstract or personified.

dysteleology   Term denoting purposelessness in nature.

E   One of the four main sources of the Pentateuch, written by the *Elohist*, so called because of his use of the word *elohim* for God. Less extensive but close in form to J (q.v.), it was probably written later in the Northern Kingdom, about the 8th cent. BC, but was edited in quite early (JE, q.v.) and cannot be easily distinguished.

'ebed   (Hebrew) 'Servant'.

'Ebed YHWH 'The Servant of the LORD' – the SUFFERING SERVANT of Deutero-Isaiah.

Ebionites Ascetic Jewish-Christian sect that flourished east of Jordan in the 2nd cent.; noted for a 'low' Christology and emphasis on the Mosaic law.

Ebionites, Gospel of the See HEBREWS, GOSPEL OF THE.

Ecce homo (Latin) 'Behold the man!', Jn. 19.5.

ecclesia See EKKLESIA.

Ecclesiastes (Ecc.) Pessimistic reflections on the inscrutability of God and the vanity of the world, from the encounter between the Jewish Wisdom tradition and echoes of Greek philosophy; probably 3rd cent. BC.

Ecclesiastical Text Occasional extra name for the BYZANTINE TEXT.

Ecclesiasticus See SIRACH.

ecclesiology Doctrine of the Church.

eclecticism Combining of the 'best' elements from a number of different faiths or theologies.

economy The divine government of the world, particularly in relation to man's salvation. (Greek: *oikonomia*)

editio princeps (Latin) First printed edition of an ancient text.

Egerton Papyrus (P. Eg. 2) Greek fragments of a non-canonical gospel written in Egypt before AD 150. First published as *An Unknown Gospel*.

Egyptian Text Occasional name for the ALEXANDRIAN TEXT.

Egyptians, Gospel of the Greek gospel of the early 2nd cent. extant only in a few quotations. Compiled by Gentile Christians of the Nile Delta, it shows gnostic and encratite tendencies. Not to be confused with the Book of the GREAT INVISIBLE SPIRIT, which is given the same name in its colophon.

Eighteen Benedictions (Hebrew: *Shemoneh-Esreh*) Form of daily Jewish prayer for personal and synagogue use, the bulk of which was fixed by the 1st cent. AD.

eirenic Pacific, encouraging peace.

eisegesis Reading one's own interpretation into a text; pejorative term for improper EXEGESIS.

ekklesia (Greek) 'Church', 'assembly'.

Elchasai, Book of Collection of instructions and apocalyptic prophecies written by the Jewish-Christian Elchasaite sect, somewhere east of the Jordan in the first years of the 2nd cent.; known only from quotations.

Eldad and Medad, Book of   Jewish apocryphon no longer extant based on Num. 11.26–9.

Elephantine Papyri   Aramaic letters and legal documents of the 5th cent. BC (during the Persian period) from a Jewish military colony on the Nile in Upper Egypt, notable for its syncretistic worship of Yahu with other gods at its own temple.

Elijah Cycle   I Kg. 17–19; 21; II Kg. 1. Dramatic, beautifully constructed stories about the prophet Elijah, probably written in prophetic circles in the Northern Kingdom at the end of the 9th cent. BC.

Elisha Cycle   II Kg. 2–13. Stories about Elisha the prophet; influenced by the ELIJAH CYCLE, they were probably written by prophets of the Northern Kingdom in the 8th cent. BC.

elohim   (Hebrew) 'God'. A plural of majesty, it can if not referring to the LORD himself mean 'gods'.

Elohist   Name given to the unknown author or authors of E (q.v.).

Elohist Psalter   Pss. 42–83. Early collection of Psalms, so called because of the use of ELOHIM when addressing God; it is made up of presumably earlier collections, the first group of *Korahite Psalms*, 42–9, the *Second Davidic Psalter*, 51–72, and the *Psalms of Asaph*, 50, 73–83.

enchorial   Occasional synonym for DEMOTIC.

enclitic   Word so unemphasized that its accent is pushed back onto the preceding word.

encratite   Title given to several early Christian sects, such as the Ebionites, Gnostics and Docetists, noted for their extreme asceticism, which included a rejection of wine, meat and marriage.

endogamy   Custom whereby a man has to marry a woman from within his own tribe; the opposite of EXOGAMY.

Endzeit   (German) The 'end-time', the ESCHATON.

energumen   Someone possessed by a devil.

Enoch, Books of
   I Ethiopic Enoch   A composite work from several

authors, writing from the 2nd cent. BC to the 1st cent. AD, it is the most significant book of the Pseudepigrapha. Written in Hebrew and/or Aramaic and incorporating the Book of NOAH, it had considerable influence on the Qumran community and the NT writers. 108 chapters long, some of the most important are:

37–71, the *Parables* or *Similitudes*, containing the much disputed references to the Son of Man and the Elect One, of the early 1st cent. AD, which could be either Jewish or Christian.

72–82, the Book of the *Heavenly Luminaries*, a Wisdom treatise on cosmology and certainly one of the earliest sections.

83–90, the *Dream Visions*, concerning the Flood and an allegorical interpretation of history.

91–105, an *Epistle* of exhortation and admonition, including 93, an *Apocalypse of Weeks*, a schematization of world history in which seven weeks have passed and three are yet to come; with chs. 1–36 it may have formed the first draft of the Book.

II Slavonic Enoch or **Book of the Secrets of Enoch** Cosmology, history and ethics, with similarities to, but no literary dependence upon, I Enoch. Written in Greek in the 1st cent. AD or later, it could be either Jewish or Christian.

III Anti-Christian Hebrew apocalypse of about the 3rd cent. AD.

Enthronement Festival Suggested festival of the first Jerusalem Temple, in which YHWH was proclaimed as King and the Davidic dynasty reaffirmed; evidence is found in certain of the Psalms, e.g. 2, 21, 72, 89, 110.

Entmythologisierung German for DEMYTHOLOGIZATION.

Enuma Elish Akkadian creation epic of the Old Babylonian period (early 2nd millenium), recited on the fourth day of the New Year festival; it recalls the birth of the gods, the battle in which the god Marduk defeats the monster of chaos Tiamat, and the creation of the world.

eparch Governor or prefect in charge of a province.

epexegesis Elucidation of a phrase or sentence of Scripture by the addition of a word or words.

Ephesians (Eph.) Very close to Colossians, it could have been written by Paul when in prison in the early 60s, but is more likely to have been a deutero-pauline text, of the 80s?, based on Colossians.

Ephraimite Source Occasional, alternative name for E.

epiclesis Invocation of the Holy Spirit; strictly within the Eucharistic prayer, but often used more generally.

epigone One of a succeeding and lesser generation.

epigraphy Study of inscriptions.

epimyth The moral that follows a fable.

epinicion (Greek) A song composed to celebrate a particular victory; e.g. Ex. 15 or Jg. 5.

epiphany (Greek) 'Manifestation' of God. More general in application than THEOPHANY, it is, wisely, not often used in biblical studies.

epiphora In literary analysis, the repetition of a concluding word or phrase; e.g. '. . . under the law', I Cor. 9.20.

epistemology That branch of philosophy that deals with the nature and validity of knowledge.

Epistula Apostolorum Unusual Christian apocryphon recounting the conversations between the Apostles and Christ after his resurrection, written in pseudo-gnostic style by a Catholic to combat the growing threat of Gnosticism; Greek, *c.* 150.

epithalamion (Greek) A wedding song; e.g. Ps. 45 or S. of S. 3.6–11.

eponymy Giving one's name to a place or institution; e.g. 'Israel', 'God of Abraham'.

erchomenos, ho (Greek) 'He who comes'. Almost a title of Jesus in John's Gospel.

Eretz Israel Modern Hebrew name for 'the Land of Israel'.

eros (Greek) 'Passionate love'; not used by the NT writers, see AGAPE.

Erweiswort (German) 'Proof saying', 'saying of self-attestation', by which the LORD reveals his power and authority; e.g. I Kg. 20.13.

eschatology Doctrine of the last things, such as the end of the world, the establishment of the Kingdom of God and the messianic age. Hence *eschatological* relates to any teaching, writing etc. that includes this perspective of the imminent end of the present age and the inauguration of the reign of God.

eschaton   (Greek) 'The end (of the world)'.

Esdras   Greek and Latin form of the name EZRA.

Essenes   Jewish sect within Palestine, pious, disciplined, monastic and often celibate, who were active between the 2nd cent. BC and the 2nd cent. AD; not mentioned in the Bible or the Talmud, their precise extent is not clear, though some identification with the Qumran community is now evident.

Esther   (Est.) Legend of a triumph over anti-semitism set in the Persian period, with no concern for any specifically religious matters and no mention of God. Written probably in the 3rd cent. BC to commend the observance of the festival of Purim among the Jews of Palestine. Several additions to the book, supplying a more religious perspective, are found in the Greek translation and now make up a section of the Apocrypha.

et al.   (Latin) 'And others'; the equivalent of *etc.* when used of people.

ethnarch   Ruler of a people.

ethnography   Scientific description of different peoples and their characteristics.

etiology   See AETIOLOGY.

euangelion   (Greek) 'Gospel'.

Eugnostos the Blessed, Epistle of   See SOPHIA JESU CHRISTI.

euhemerism   Theory put forward in the 4th cent. that the ancient stories about the gods are in fact elaborations of real incidents in human history.

eulogia   (Greek) 'Blessing'.

Eusebian Canons   Set of ten tables of numbers, based on the AMMONIAN SECTIONS and devised by Eusebius (*c.* 400), to indicate parallel passages in the Gospels.

Euthalian Apparatus   Editorial notes and divisions, possibly 4th cent., found in some Greek manuscripts of Acts and the Epistles.

Evangelium Veritatis   Less common name for the Gospel of TRUTH.

excursus   Detailed discussion of some technical point not covered in the main body of the text, added in the form of an appendix.

Execration Texts Egyptian tablets, 20th to 18th cent. BC, on which curses directed against particular people were written; they were then broken to effect the curse.

exegesis The systematic explanation and interpretation of a biblical text. Just exactly *how* a biblical text is to be interpreted and explained is rather more the concern of HERMENEUTICS.

exegete One who performs EXEGESIS.

existentialism 20th cent. philosophical school or approach that lays greatest stress on subjective existence, experience and commitment, in the here and now. A fundamental category of analysis that it places on all human activity is that between authentic and inauthentic, or in theology between faith and unfaith.

Exodus (Ex.) Chs. 1–18, freedom from the bondage of Egypt and journey to Sinai; 19–40, giving of the Sinai covenant and its laws, including the Book of the COVENANT. Composed of J, E and P, the events took place some time during the XIXth Egyptian Dynasty, 1350–1200 BC.

exogamy Custom whereby a man has to marry a woman from outside his own tribe; the opposite of ENDOGAMY.

exomologesis (Greek) Full, public confession of sins.

ex opere operato (Latin) Phrase used for the doctrine that a sacrifice or sacrament is fully effective if its form is validly fulfilled irrespective of the worth of the person administering or receiving it.

The less common phrase *ex opere operantis* denotes the contrary view that it *is* dependent on the performer.

exordium Introductory section of a treatise.

exousia (Greek) 'Authority', 'right', 'power'.

expiation Atonement or making reparation for an offence, usually made against God.

explicandum (Latin) That which is to be explained.

explicatio (Latin) The explanation, the aetiology.

ex post facto (Latin) Retrospective.

extra-canonical Outside the CANON; not belonging to or found in the Bible.

Ezekiel (Ezek.) A priest and a prophet, he preached to his fellow exiles in Babylon from 593 BC before the final destruction of Jerusalem, to 571. In more or less chronological order, chs, 1–24, oracles of warning; 25–32, oracles against the nations; 33–9, oracles of hope for restoration; 40–8, vision of the new Jerusalem temple and community, in which he shows similarities to the PRIESTLY SOURCE. Notable too for his fantastic visions that prefigure those of APOCALYPTIC.

Ezra (Ezr.) Not to be confused with the books mentioned below. Part of the larger work of the CHRONICLER. Ezra is generally reckoned to have returned *c.* 400 BC with a book of Mosaic law, perhaps P, and to have established the religious, legal framework for the community at Jerusalem, a framework that became the basis of Judaism as a whole. The text is, along with that of Nehemiah, severely disrupted; a suggested reconstruction in chronological order is as follows: Ezr. 1.1–11; 2.1–70 (= Neh. 7.6–73a); 3.1–4.6; 4.24–6.22; 4.7–23; Neh. 1.1–7.5; 11.1–13.30; 9.38–10.39; Ezr. 7.1–10.44; Neh. 8.1–9.37. No solution, however, is entirely free from objections.

Ezra, Books of Ezra and Nehemiah were known in Latin Bibles as the 1st and 2nd books of Esdras, but two books of Esdras are also found in the Apocrypha (though not among the deuterocanonical books). This has led to more than a little confusion in the numbering: the 3rd book can become the 1st, the 4th the 2nd, though the 5th and 6th remain the same, unless reckoned as part of the 2nd (or 4th).

III Greek Ezra (I Esd.) Greek rewriting of the 1st or 2nd cent. BC of the last two chapters of II Chronicles, the whole of Ezra and part of chs. 7–8 of Nehemiah, into which has been inserted the Story of the THREE YOUNG MEN. Quite how this version came about is not clear but its aim was to heighten the importance of Josiah, Zerubbabel and Ezra in the reform of Israel's worship.

IV Ezra Apocalypse (II Esd. 3–14) A series of apocalyptic visions given to Ezra. Written in Hebrew though extant only in translations, *c.* 100 AD, it sought to apply the lessons learnt from the fall of Jerusalem in 587 BC to the suffering and despair following the fall of AD 70.

V (II Esd. 1–2) Christian addition to the *Ezra Apocalypse*, in Greek *c.* 200.

VI (II Esd. 15–16) Another Christian addition to the same work, in Greek late 3rd cent.

f/ff   And the following verse/verses or page/pages etc.

family   Group of manuscripts, usually Greek MINUSCULES of the NT, that show a marked similarity of text, which suggests a shared origin; a much smaller group of manuscripts than a TEXT-TYPE.

Family 1   See LAKE GROUP.

Family 13   See FERRAR GROUP.

Farewell Discourses   Jn. 13.31–16.33. Jesus's speeches to his disciples at the Last Supper.

fascicule   Section of a larger book, or volume of books.

Fathers   The early Christian theologians, from the 2nd cent. onwards. Also known more fully as the *Church Fathers*, or subdivided into the *Greek Fathers* and the *Latin Fathers*. ·

Fathers, Jewish   Name, now rare, for the Rabbis who compiled the MISHNAH.

Fayyum Fragment   Seven line fragment of a 3rd cent. AD Greek papyrus found in Egypt, seemingly an abridgement of the prediction of Peter's denial.

Fayyumic   COPTIC dialect spoken in the Fayyum Oasis; texts date from the 4th to the 11th cent.

Ferrar Group   Group of NT MINUSCULES, probably from Calabria in southern Italy from the 11th cent. onwards, known also as *Family 13*, reflecting the CAESAREAN TEXT.

Festperikopen   (German) 'Cultic narratives'.

Festschrift   (German) Collection of essays written, usually by his former students or colleagues, for the birthday of a renowned scholar.

fiat   (Latin) 'Let it be.' A creative command; e.g. 'Let there be light', Gen. 1.3.

fides historica   Conventional, inherited religious beliefs of one's social and cultural group, as distinct from a living, personal faith of one's own.

figura etymologica   An etymological pun; much used in Genesis, e.g. the names of Jacob's sons, chs. 29–30.

fl.   (Latin: *floruit*) 'He flourished'; indicating the date when a person was known to be active, when those of his birth and death remain unknown.

floating logion   A short saying of Jesus found in different contexts within the gospels; e.g. 'The first shall be last, . . .'.

Flood Tablet   Tablet XI of the Epic of GILGAMESH.

florilegium   (Modern Latin) An anthology, in particular of OT proof texts as used by early Christians.

fons et origo   (Latin) 'Source and origin'.

form criticism   Study of the source and history of biblical texts by analysing their structural form and relating this to their origin and transmission within the community. In the OT one of the tasks is to discover the ancient, often poetic, forms used for the transmission of oral tradition, the influence of the religious or social setting in which they would have been recited and how they would have changed and developed over the centuries up to, and after, being written down. A major task in the NT is to discover the classic forms of speech that Jesus used in teaching, such as the parable, and how they came to be expanded and elaborated when used by the early Church in its own preaching and teaching.

Former Prophets   Title in the Hebrew canon for the historical books of the OT: Joshua, Judges, Samuel, Kings.

Formgeschichte   German for FORM CRITICISM.

four source hypothesis   A solution to the SYNOPTIC PROBLEM that elaborates on the TWO SOURCE HYPOTHESIS. It suggests four independent early documents, M, Mark, Q and L; Matthew used the first three sources when compiling his own gospel, Luke the last three. (B. Streeter)

fragment hypothesis   19th cent. theory that rejected the possibility of there being continuous narrative sources within the Pentateuch, and argued rather for many, short, independent fragments of local tradition.

fratriarchal   Relating to a society where the brother has greater legal authority over a woman than her husband; e.g. Gen. 12.10ff (perhaps!).

Freer Logion   Prophetic words of Christ added at Mk. 16.14, found only in the 5th cent. Greek codex 'W'.

Frühkatholizismus   (German) The emergent CATHOLIC character of the early Church.

fundamentalism   Reactionary movement of this century, characterized by Anglo-Saxon, Protestant values, that rejects the whole of modern biblical scholarship and insists on the complete inerrancy of the Bible. Often used in a general and pejorative sense, it is also synonymous with *conservative evangelicalism*.

G (From GRUNDLAGE) Oldest narrative source or tradition in the Pentateuch, behind both J and E (qq.v.); seemingly 12th or 11th cent. BC, though dating is virtually impossible. (M. Noth)

Galatians (Gal.) Written by Paul to that Church when under threat from JUDAIZERS. Chs. 1–2 contain many autobiographical details that seem to differ from the facts recorded in Acts. Various dates in the 50s have been argued.

Gamma Recent designation for the text-type more commonly known as the CAESAREAN TEXT.

Gattung (German) 'Genre'; also 'class', 'type', 'family'. In practice a literary unit such as a gospel or apocalypse, and larger than a *form* which is usually oral at least in origin.

Gattungsforschung (German) 'Study of genres'.

Gattungsgeschichte (German) 'History of genres'. Usually synonymous with FORM CRITICISM.

Gehenna Ravine south of Jerusalem that was once a place of human sacrifice; in NT times used metaphorically for the place of punishment in the next life, a far nastier place than either HADES or SHEOL.

Geist (German) 'Spirit'; often in compounds, such as *Weltgeist*, 'spirit of the age'.

Geistesbeschäftigung (German) 'Way of thinking', 'attitude of mind'.

Gemara (Aramaic) 'Tradition'. Name given to the second part of the TALMUD; the commentary in Aramaic by the AMORAIM on the first part, the MISHNAH.

gematria Interpretation of hidden meaning within a text by adding up the numerical values of the letters of key words; note Rev. 13.18 (666).

Gemeindeordnungen or **Gemeinderegeln** (German) Discipline and regulations of the early churches.

General Epistles Another name for the CATHOLIC EPISTLES.

Genesis (Gen.) Chs. 1–11, primeval history from the creation of the world; 12–36, the stories of the patriarchs Abraham, Isaac and Jacob; 37–50, mainly the JOSEPH STORY. Composed of J, E and P and/or even earlier sources such as G.

Genesis Apocryphon Aramaic fragments from Qumran,

containing a popular, expanded account of Noah and of Abram and Sarai.

genetic fallacy Error, to which historical criticism is prone, of supposing that to trace a text back to its origins is to understand it.

geniza Room attached to a synagogue for the storing of worn-out copies of Scripture, and thus a valuable source of ancient manuscripts. The most famous is the *Cairo Geniza* discovered in 1896 and containing fragments dating back to AD 882.

Geonim Jewish intellectual leaders and transmitters of the tradition, in Babylonia from the 6th to the 11th cent., succeeding the SAVORAIM.

ger (Hebrew) 'Sojourner', 'resident alien'; perhaps originally a nomad living within the area of a settled society, such as Abraham, Gen. 23.4.

Gerichtsrede (German) 'Lawsuit'.

Geschichte (German; adjective: *geschichtlich*) 'History', meaning that which is historic and significant but also unverifiable; e.g. the assertion that the Lord brought his people out of Egypt. As opposed to HISTORIE, the merely historical.

Gezer Calendar Small soft-stone tablet in early Hebrew, *c.* 1000 BC, containing a list of eight months and their related agricultural activity.

Gilgamesh, Epic of Epic poem on twelve tablets concerning Gilgamesh, the partly divine ruler of Uruk, a powerful treatment of love and friendship, struggle and adventure, and behind it all the inevitable approach of death. Written in Akkadian, early in the 2nd millenium BC it has reworked and developed even older Sumerian sources. Tablet XI contains an account of the Great Flood, often referred to as the *Babylonian Flood Narrative*.

glacis Steep slope leading up to the walls of a city.

Gleichnisse (German) 'Similitudes', parabolic sayings.

gloss A short comment, explanation or interpretation inserted into a text by some later writer or scribe.

glossator Writer of a GLOSS.

glossolalia Gift of speaking in tongues, as at Pentecost.

gnomic From the less common noun *gnome*, a general maxim or aphorism.

gnosis (Greek) 'Knowledge', referring to a special, often secret, knowledge of the spiritual mysteries.

Gnosticism General term for a large number of semi-Christian sects, at their height in the 2nd and 3rd centuries, that were founded on a secret tradition or GNOSIS. Though the different groups varied widely in their complex and hierarchical cosmologies and mythologies, they shared in common the offer of spiritual salvation to the individual (and freedom from the material world) by means of this special knowledge. The origins and influences are much debated: Christianity certainly, sectarian Judaism probably, eastern religions possibly.

In general *Gnostic* is used to refer to the sects, *gnostic* to the general tendencies, evident even in the NT.

go'el (Hebrew) 'Next of kin', 'protector', 'avenger (of blood)'.

Golden Rule Modern name for Christ's precept of Mt. 7.12, 'Always treat others as you would like them to treat you.'

Gottesdienst (German) 'Worship'.

goyim (Hebrew) 'Nations, 'Gentiles'.

Graf–Wellhausen hypothesis Theory of the literary development of the Pentateuch that has commanded the widest general assent this century; it asserts four main sources, which were written and combined in the following chronological order: J, E, (JE), D, (JED), P, (JEDP).

Great Invisible Spirit, Book of the Coptic treatise from Nag Hammadi, also given the inaccurate title Gospel of the EGYPTIANS.

Grecian Age Later name for the SELEUCID ERA.

Greek See KOINE.

Griesbach hypothesis Theory that Mark was the last of the three Synoptic Gospels to be written and is dependent on both Matthew and Luke, of which it is a conflation. Named after J. Griesbach who first proposed this view in 1783.

Grundlage (German) Foundation tradition; underlying oral source. See also G.

Grundschrift (German) The same as GRUNDLAGE, only written.

H Designation of the HOLINESS CODE.

Habakkuk (Hab.) Chs. 1–2.5, a dialogue between the prophet and God; 2.6–20, the five woes; 3, a hymn in praise of God, perhaps very ancient. Habakkuk, the author of possibly only the first section, prophesied *c.* 600 BC.

Habakkuk Commentary (1QpHab) Qumran commentary on Hab. 1–2, of the 1st cent. BC, that relates the conflict between the TEACHER OF RIGHTEOUSNESS and the Wicked Priest, and the arrival of the 'Kittim' (probably the Roman army) in Palestine.

Habiru (Or *Hapiru*, or *Apiru*.) People mentioned in a very wide number of texts from the 2nd millenium BC; possibly refugees, social outcasts or nomadic tribesmen, there is no consensus as to their exact identity, though some sort of connection with the early Hebrews who entered Canaan still seems probable.

Hades (Greek) The dwelling-place of departed spirits. It translates the Hebrew *Sheol*, and is not the equivalent of *Hell* if reckoned as the place of punishment (for which see GEHENNA).

hadith (Arabic) Sayings and stories of Mohammed in the oral transmission of early Islam, often compared with early Christian traditions.

Haggadah (Hebrew) 'Narrative'. That part of post-biblical rabbinic writing that is not HALAKHAH, in other words non-prescriptive, consisting of legends, stories, parables and folk-lore.

Haggai (Hag.) Preaching in Jerusalem in 520 BC he, along with Zechariah, urged the people to complete the rebuilding of the Temple that had been neglected, and promised great blessing when it was achieved.

Hagiographa (Greek) 'Sacred Writings'. Title of the third section of the Hebrew Bible, i.e. not the Law nor the Prophets. Also known as *The Writings* or by the Hebrew name *Ketubim*.

hagiography The writing of the lives of saints.

hakhamim (Hebrew) 'Sages', 'wise men'.

Halakhah The legal, prescriptive part of post-biblical Jewish tradition. The main study of the Scribes, Rabbis and later

77

teachers, for whom it was the supreme religious duty, it was and is of much greater importance than HAGGADAH.

Hallel (Hebrew) 'Praise'. Title of Pss. 113–18; sometimes called the *Egyptian Hallel*.

Hammurabi, Code of The finest of the pre-Israelite law codes, comprising 282 laws, CASUISTIC in style, with a long prologue and epilogue; written in Akkadian *c.* 1700 BC, during the reign of Hammurabi of the Old Babylonian (Amorite) dynasty.

hapaxlegomenon (Greek) 'Something said only once'. A word that occurs only once in ancient literature: its meaning cannot therefore be checked from another context.

haphtorah (Hebrew) A portion from the NEBIIM for public reading in synagogue after the reading from the TORAH. (Plural: *haphtaroth*)

haplography Copyist's unintentional writing of a letter or word only once where it ought to be repeated. Opposite error to DITTOGRAPHY.

Harklean Version Revision of the PHILOXENIAN Syriac Version of the NT, by Thomas of Harkel in 616, that included variant readings in the margin, which are a major witness to the WESTERN TEXT.

Hasidim (Hebrew) 'Saints'. Name of a group of Jews in the time of the Maccabees and after; pious, conservative and intensely faithful even in the face of persecution, they were the precursors of the Pharisees.

Haustafeln German for HOUSEHOLD CODES.

Havdalah Jewish blessing recited at the end of Sabbaths and festivals.

hazzan (Hebrew) Minister of synagogue worship, similar to the Christian deacon.

Heavenly Luminaries, Book of the See I ENOCH.

hebraica veritas (Latin) Phrase of Jerome for the true and original Hebrew text of the OT, as opposed to mere Greek translation.

Hebrew One of the north-western Semitic group of languages. Alphabetical texts are known from the 10th cent. BC. It was gradually superseded by Aramaic from the 5th cent. BC onwards, and in the Diaspora by Greek from the 3rd cent. BC onwards.

Hebrews (Heb.) Highly individual treatise by an unknown Jewish Christian, in good Greek, underlining the nature of the redemption worked by Christ in terms of OT prophecy and Jewish ritual; late 60s.

Hebrews, Gospel of the This has presented scholars with a most difficult problem, aggravated by several confusing statements by Jerome. Although some books still assume there to have been only one work, there are now generally reckoned to have been three such gospels, all from the early 2nd cent.:

Gospel of the Nazarenes An Aramaic targum from Coelesyria of the Greek text of Matthew, used by the sect of that name.

Gospel of the Ebionites Based on the Synoptics and used by the sect of that name; Greek, from east of the Jordan.

Gospel of the Hebrews In Greek from Egypt; either based on the canonical gospels or from an early, independent tradition.

The evidence amounts to only a few quotations in each case, and many scholars still equate one with another. All that is certain is that at present no other Jewish-Christian Gospels are reckoned to have existed.

hecatomb Large, public sacrifice of a great numbers of animals.

hegemony Leadership or domination of one state over another without actual direct rule or occupation.

Heilsgeschichte (German) 'Salvation history'. The mighty acts of God in history.

Hellenization The encroachment and domination of the Greek language and thought over the peoples and cultures of the eastern Mediterranean, including, of course, the Jews, especially those living outside Palestine, from the conquests of Alexander the Great onwards. This shared basis of Greek thought away from Greece itself is called Hellenism.

hendiadys (Greek) 'One through two'. Figure of speech in which two words are joined by a conjunction, rather than one subordinated to the other; e.g. I Pet. 1.3, 'Blessed be the God *and* Father of our Lord Jesus Christ', rather than '. . . the God *who is* the Father of our Lord Jesus Christ'.

henotheism   Faith in one God, without actually asserting that he is the only God.

heortology   That part of ecclesiology that deals with religious festivals.

Heptateuch   Scholars' name for the first seven books of the OT, Genesis–Judges, when regarded as a unit.

herem   (Hebrew) 'Ban', 'anathema'. The law of total destruction of the enemy and all his property during the Holy War.

heresiarch   Founder of a heretical sect.

heresiologue   Writer who records the teachings of heretics, usually to combat their doctrines. Until the major discoveries of the last two centuries, in particular that at Nag Hammadi, our main source of information on Gnostics and other early Christian heretical sects were such writers as Irenaeus and Epiphanius.

heretical   That which departs from or denies what is correct and orthodox. In biblical studies it is generally applied to Christian sects, while HETERODOX is used in Jewish contexts, and used more as a historical judgement, that those ideas *were* not accepted by the main body of the Church, than as a value judgement, that those ideas *should* not have been accepted.

Hermas, Shepherd of   Repetitive and earnest work reckoned among the APOSTOLIC FATHERS, consisting of five *Visions*, revealing the character of the Church, in the last of which appears the Shepherd, twelve *Mandates*, a compilation of moral commands, and finally ten, long *Similitudes* or allegories; written in Greek, *c.* 150 AD, in Rome.

Hermeneutic, The New   Recent approach, under the influence of Heidegger, that seeks to go beyond Bultmann's demythologization, arguing that language, and therefore the language of the gospel, is the instrument by which reality comes into being, and not merely the record of that reality. See LANGUAGE EVENT.

hermeneutic circle   Technical term for the realization that comprehension is necessarily circular; i.e. that one cannot understand the whole without understanding the parts, nor the parts without the whole.

hermeneutics   The interpretation and understanding of

Scripture; as it were the general art or science ('How are we to interpret the Bible?'), behind and distinct from EXEGESIS.

Hermetic literature   Popular occult writings, in Greek, of the 1st and 2nd cent. AD, supposedly by Hermes Trismegistus, being an amalgam of Egyptian religion and Greek Platonism.

hesed   (Hebrew) 'Loving-kindness', 'mercy', 'grace'.

heterodox   That which is not in accord with what is generally regarded as correct and orthodox. In biblical studies it is usually applied to Jewish sects, while HERETICAL is used in Christian contexts.

heteronomy   Ethical assertion that the moral laws are, and ought to be, imposed by some authority other than oneself; though if by God this is called THEONOMY. As opposed to AUTONOMY.

heuristic   Relating to teaching in which the listener discovers the truth for himself. Note the parables of Jesus.

hexaemeron   The six day creation of the world; Gen. 1.

Hexapla   Critical edition of the OT text produced by Origen, c. 230–45, in six parallel columns, containing the Hebrew, the Hebrew transliterated into Greek, and the Greek versions of Aquila, Symmachus, Theodotion and the Septuagint.

Hexateuch   Scholars' name for the first six books of the OT, Genesis–Joshua, when regarded as a single literary unit.

Hezekiah, Testament of   See ISAIAH, ASCENSION OF.

hic et nunc   (Latin) 'Here and now'.

hierarch   High priest.

hieratic script   Cursive form of the Egyptian HEIROGLYPHS, developed in the 3rd millenium BC for greater speed of writing on papyrus.

hieroglyphs   Pictographic symbols used in the ancient Egyptian system of writing.

hierograph   Sacred symbol.

hierology   Uncommon name for the study of the history of religions.

hierophant   Priest, or exponent, of a mystery cult.

hieros gamos   (Greek) 'Sacred marriage'. Union between god and woman, or man and goddess, often in ancient fertility ritual.

hieros logos (Greek) 'Sacred word'. Central pronouncement or confession, from which further traditions develop.

higher criticism Name, now rarely used, for the study of forms and sources within the biblical texts, as distinct from the LOWER (TEXTUAL) CRITICISM.

High Priestly Prayer Jn. 17. Jesus's prayer to the Father, which immediately follows the FAREWELL DISCOURSES.

hilasterion (Greek) 'A means of expiation', Rom. 3.25; 'the mercy-seat'. (Hebrew: KAPPORETH)

historical criticism Broad term for the main body of modern biblical scholarship, that seeks to understand the texts within the historical circumstances of the time in which they were written and transmitted.

Historie (German; adjective: *historisch*) 'History', meaning that which is historical and objectively verifiable; e.g. that a group of Semitic slaves may have escaped from Egypt *c.* 1250 BC. As opposed to GESCHICHTE, that which is historic.

historiography The writing of history.

History of Religions School See RELIGIONSGESCHICHTLICHE SCHULE.

Hittite Indo-European language of the Hittite Empire; in cuneiform from 1600 BC to 1200 BC and in hieroglyphs in the southern part of the empire, 1600 BC to 700 BC.

Hodayoth (Hebrew) 'Thanksgiving' psalms and praises, particularly those from Qumran.

Holiness Code (H) Lev. 17–26. Collection of Mosaic legislation, mainly cultic in character and laying great stress on holiness 'for I the LORD am holy'. Written by priests and probably completed *c.* 550 BC, it was later incorporated into P (q.v.).

holocaust From the Greek for 'wholly burn'. In biblical studies, a sacrifice completely consumed by fire.

homiletics Art or science of preaching.

homoioteleuton (Greek) 'Similar ending'. Copying error, usually of omission, caused by two words with similar endings close together or on adjacent lines.

homoioarcton ('Similar beginning') is the same error caused by similar beginnings of words, but since this is much less frequent, the term is rare.

homologumena Works of undisputed authorship; used especially of Paul's letters.

homology Less common term for a confession or affirmation of faith.

homoousios (Greek) 'Of the same substance'. A key patristic term, as distinguished from *homoiousios*, 'of like substance'.

Hosea (Hos.) The only written prophet from the Northern Kingdom, he preached shortly after Amos, *c.* 730 BC. Through his own experience with his faithless wife Gomer, he condemned the harlotry and adultery of Baal worship and proclaimed the enduring and redeeming love of the Lord even in a context of punishment.

household codes Collections of ethical rules relating to husbands and wives, parents and children, masters and slaves, characteristic of the hierarchical society of the Mediterranean in NT times; e.g. Eph. 5.21–6.9.

hubris (Greek) 'Arrogance', 'pride'; the classic human sin.

Humash (Hebrew) 'Five fifths'. Title of the PENTATEUCH.

Hurrian Non-Semitic language brought from the north in 2nd millenium BC invasions, and with considerable influence on HEBREW and other north-western Semitic languages.

hylic (From the Greek for 'wood') In Gnostic thought that which is material. Opposite of PNEUMATIC.

hylozoism Doctrine of the Greeks that all matter is endowed with life.

hypocoristic name Compound name that has been shortened; in the OT it is often the divine epithet that is dropped; e.g. 'Ahaz' from 'Jehoahaz', or 'Adon' from 'Adonijah'.

hypostasis Greek word for 'substance' but with far richer meaning. In Christology usually translated as 'person' or 'being'. Hence the verb *hypostasize*, or *hypostatize*, to make into a person or substance; e.g. Wisdom in Pr. 8.

hypotaxis Opposite literary style to PARATAXIS: the elaboration or excess of syntactical relations between clauses; a characteristic of Paul's writing, under Greek rather than Semitic influence.

hypotheses Brief introductions to the books of the Bible, found in some manuscripts, giving details of the author, content and circumstances of composition.

Ialdabaoth   Gnostic corruption of the Hebrew title 'Yahweh Sabaoth',applied to the inferior DEMIURGE.

iambic   (Hebrew poetry) Metre of one unstressed syllable followed by one stressed.

ibid.   (Latin) Of a reference from a book or text, 'in the same place'.

Icthus   (Greek for 'fish') Early Christian cryptogram whose Greek letters spell out the initials of 'Jesus Christ Son of God Saviour'.

id.   (Latin: *idem*) 'The same'.

ideogram or **ideograph**   Written character symbolizing the idea of a thing without expressing its name – as in Chinese or the earliest writing.

Ignatius, Epistles of   Seven letters, included among the APOSTOLIC FATHERS, written by Ignatius, bishop of Antioch in the late 1st and early 2nd cent., when on his way to martyrdom in Rome. Warning against JUDAIZERS and DOCETISM, he reveals an intense faith based on a living tradition and the growing spiritual importance of the bishop.

ignoratio elenchi   (Latin) The error of proving or disproving something other than what was in question.

imago Dei   (Latin) 'Image of God'; Gen. 1.27.

immanence   The actual presence, the indwelling, of God in his created world. Contrasted with TRANSCENDENCE.

Immanuel, Book of   Occasional name for Is. 6–12.

immolation   Strictly the sprinkling of a sacrificial victim with meal; more generally, the slaughtering of the victim.

inclusio   (Latin) Poetic passage where the opening theme or phrase is returned to at the end.

ineffable   That which cannot be expressed in words.

in extenso   (Latin) At full length; word for word.

infancy narratives   Mt. 1–2 and Lk. 1–2; generally reckoned among the latest elements of the gospel tradition.

in limine   (Latin) 'On the threshold'; at the outset.

in perpetuo   (Latin) 'For all time'.

insufflation   The breathing upon a person in the giving of the Holy Spirit; from Jn. 20.22.

intellective horizon   The historical and cultural limits to one's intellectual understanding.

inter alia   (Latin) 'Among other things'. For people it should be '*inter alios/alias*', or better still avoided.

intercalary month   Extra month, called Ve-Adar, added every two or three years at the end of the Jewish lunar year, to bring it into harmony with the solar year. So by extension *intercalary* may mean any insertion or interpolation.

interim ethic   Term applied to the teaching of Jesus, arguing that it was given in the expectation of the imminent end of the present world order; it cannot, therefore, be directly applied to our own age and situation.

interpolation   Later insertion of material into a text; something longer than a GLOSS.

intertextuality   Necessary relationship any literary text must have with other texts, from which it can never be entirely free.

in vacuo   (Latin) 'In a vacuum'.

Iosue   Latin form of JOSHUA.

ipse dixit   (Latin) 'He himself said it'. An unproved assertion, with no other authority than that of the speaker.

ipsissima verba   (Latin) 'The very word itself'. Applied in particular to Jesus, it refers to his actual words, as distinct from sayings attributed to him by the early Church. Since most scholars would argue that this is rarely obtainable from the gospel texts, however careful one's investigation, one must seek the IPSISSIMA VOX.

ipsissima vox   (Latin) 'The very voice itself'. The authentic message or teaching if not the actual, original words. See IPSISSIMA VERBA.

ipso facto   (Latin) 'By the fact itself'; automatically.

ira Dei   (Latin) 'The wrath of God'.

irenic   See EIRENIC.

Isaiah   (Is.) Isaiah the son of Amoz, often referred to as *First Isaiah* or *Isaiah of Jerusalem*, prophesied to the king and people of that city from *c.* 740 to *c.* 700 BC, while Judah lay under the threat of the Assyrian Empire which conquered the Northern Kingdom. The key to his message comes in his call, the Temple theophany of ch. 6, 'Holy, Holy, Holy: Lord God Almighty'; he preached the utter transcendence and power of the God of Israel and the total faith that this demanded.

Of the passages that do not belong to his writings, chs.

24–7 make up the ISAIAH APOCALYPSE, 33–5 a post-exilic addition, 36–9 the ISAIAH SOURCE, 40–55 DEUTERO-ISAIAH, 56–66 TRITO-ISAIAH.

Isaiah Apocalypse Is. 24–7. A post-exilic interpolation dating from around the 3rd cent. BC, consisting of eschatological prophecies or what is known as PROTO-APOCALYPTIC.

Isaiah, Ascension of Pseudepigraph combining three earlier sources:

    Martyrdom of Isaiah (Chs. 1–5) Jewish midrash, not later than the 1st cent. AD, on II Kg. 21.16, recounting the evil deeds of Manasseh, and Isaiah's death by being sawn in two.

    Testament of Hezekiah (3.14–4.18, interpolated in the first section) Short Christian apocalypse of the late 1st or early 2nd cent.

    Vision of Isaiah (Chs. 6–11) Description of the prophet's ascent into the heavens and the visions granted him, including an interpolated birth narrative (11.2–22); possibly Gnostic, late 2nd cent.

Isaiah Source Legends developed by his disciples, 7th cent. BC, found in II Kg. 18.13–20.19, and later also incorporated into Isaiah as chs. 36–9.

itacism Strictly, the reduction in Greek, over the passage of time, of certain long vowels to iota. By extension, the reduction of any long vowel to a short one. So also, the copyist's error of writing a single vowel for a diphthong, or vice versa.

Itala Another name for the OLD LATIN VERSIONS.

'itture sopherim (Hebrew) 'Omissions of the scribes'. Minor, pre-MASSORETIC, omissions from the Hebrew text of the OT; the only instances mentioned in the Talmud are suppressions of the conjunction *waw*.

Iudices Latin form of JUDGES.

J Early Israelite history from the creation of the world to the entry into Canaan, written by the *Yahwist*, so called because he uses the divine name from the beginning. It drew together earlier traditions into a sustained national epic (that many former scholars reckoned to have gone up to the time of Solomon) and was undoubtedly the earliest of the four main Pentateuchal sources. Written in Judah in the 10th, or possibly 9th, cent. BC.

Jahwism A former spelling of YAHWISM.

James (Jas.) One of the Catholic Epistles. A wisdom sermon in good Greek, almost entirely moral in character and very largely compatible with Judaism, which suggests a very early date, perhaps even in the 40s. Some scholars, seeing a rejection of Paul's doctrine of justification by faith alone, date it at the end of the 1st cent., but this is rather unlikely.

James, Apocryphal Letter of Record of Christ's final discourse before the Ascension; one of the Nag Hammadi texts, it preaches contempt of the world and extols martydom; 2nd cent.?, Jewish-Christian.

James, Book of Better known as the PROTEVANGELIUM.

James, Infancy Gospel of A still rarer name for the PROTEVANGELIUM.

Jashar, Book of Early Hebrew poetic source no longer extant that recorded Joshua's command to the sun to stand still, Jos. 10.13, and David's lament over Saul and Jonathan, II Sam. 1.18.

JE The combined text of the *Yahwist* and *Elohist* sources, put together in the 7th cent. BC in the Southern Kingdom. Since the two original texts cannot always be clearly separated, the combined text is often referred to.

Jeremiah (Jer.) Beginning in 627 BC he preached throughout the reforms of Josiah and the decline and fall of Jerusalem, until taken to Egypt in about 580 BC. As shown in his *Confessions*, he suffered deeply for being caught in the widening gulf between God and his people, with the inevitable destruction that would follow; but he proclaimed his faith in ultimate restoration in the *Book of Consolation*, chs. 30–3. Much of the text is misplaced, some has been rewritten by his scribe Baruch, other parts revised by later Deuteronomic editors, and the Septuagint text differs widely from the Hebrew.

Jeremiah, Confessions of The autobiographical passages in that book, 11.18–12.6; 15.10–21; 17.14–18; 18.18–23; 20.7–18.

Jeremiah, Lamentations of See LAMENTATIONS.

87

Jeremiah, Letter of Pseudepigraphal denunciation of the worship of idols; Greek, 2nd cent. BC, though perhaps taken from a 3rd cent. Hebrew original. It sometimes appears as ch. 6 of BARUCH.

Jeremiah, Paralipomena of Rarer name for the *Rest of the Words of Baruch* or IV BARUCH.

Jeremiah, Prayer of Vulgate title for Lamentations ch. 5.

Jeremy, Epistle of Former name for the Letter of JEREMIAH.

Jeu, Two Books of Highly esoteric and complex Gnostic treatises from Egypt; Greek early 3rd cent.

Jewish-Christian Gospels Gospels of 2nd cent. Jewish (as opposed to Gentile) Christian sects, whether in Greek or Aramaic. See HEBREWS, GOSPEL OF THE.

Job Chs. 1–2 and 42.7–17, an ancient folktale from outside Israel, of supreme patience under suffering, which provided the setting for a later poetic work of about the 5th cent. BC: 3–31, speeches between Job and his three comforters, on the problem of sin and innocent suffering; 32–7, later addition of speeches by Elihu; 38.1–42.6, the Lord answers from the whirlwind.

Job, Testament of Aramaic rewriting of Job, seen here as the King of Egypt, relating his struggle with Satan and his debate with four kings; from the 1st cent. BC or perhaps later, part of it entered the Septuagint text of the canonical work after 2.9.

Joel Probably a CULT PROPHET of the Second Temple, writing in the 4th cent. BC. PROTO-APOCALYPTIC visions of a plague of locusts heralding the Day of the Lord, the outpouring of the spirit and judgement of the nations.

Johannine Adjective of 'John', most usually of the fourth evangelist.

Johannine Appendix The final chapter of John's Gospel, written later by someone other than the author of chs. 1–20.

Johannine Comma 9th cent. Trinitarian interpolation introduced into the Latin text of I Jn. 5.7.

John (Jn.) Probably the last of the gospels and clearly unique in character, while containing early traditions; perhaps written in a number of stages, a date in the 90s is now often brought forward (to the late 70s?).

John, I (I Jn.) One of the Catholic Epistles, it is rather a sermon expounding the nature of Christian love and attacking latent heresy. Generally regarded as closely connected with John's Gospel, if not actually by the same hand.

John, II and III (II & III Jn.) Two very short letters by 'the Elder', probably not the author of the Gospel or the first letter; of generally late date, perhaps the 80s.

John, Acts of Though stories and traditions about John are among the earliest and go back to the 2nd cent., it is probable that our text goes back only to the 4th. Written in Greek and strongly docetic in its propaganda, it contains some imaginative legends, lengthy preaching and the *Departure of John.*

John, Apocryphon of Coptic treatise, four copies of which occur in the NAG HAMMADI library. Dating from at least as early as the mid-2nd cent. AD, it is the most important existing example of Gnostic mythology and cosmogony, and was probably not restricted to any one sect. With a deep knowledge of Jewish traditions and with Christian elements that may be secondary, it is of considerable interest for the origins of Gnosticism.

Jonah (Jon.) Chs. 1–2, Jonah and the whale; 3–4, Jonah preaching to Nineveh. A didactic tale emphasizing God's great patience and mercy, even to Gentiles; perhaps written, in the 4th cent. BC, against the exclusivism of Ezra's policies.

Joseph and Aseneth Jewish apocryphon in Greek of the turn of the era that describes Joseph's marriage to Aseneth, the beautiful daughter of an Egyptian priest, and her conversion to faith in the living God.

Joseph Story Gen. 37, 39–47, 50. Probably originally a Wisdom story based on Egyptian models, from as early as the reign of Solomon, charting the hero's rise to power in a foreign land, thanks to his God-given wisdom.

Joshua (Jos.) Chs. 1–12, entry and conquest of the land of Canaan under the leadership of Joshua; 13–22, division of the land among the tribes; 24 (and 23), the covenant at Shechem (and its Deuteronomic revision).

Jubilees, Book of One of the most important books of the Pseudepigrapha showing the development of MIDRASH and HALAKAH in the inter-testamental period, being an elaboration of Gen. 1 to Ex. 12 presented as a revelation given to Moses on Mount Sinai. Noted for its solar calendar of 364 days and the jubilees of 49 years. It has close connections with the Qumran community; c. 140 BC, in Hebrew.

Judaizers Jewish Christians who tried to impose the full OT law and ritual upon others in the early Church; Paul's especial opponents in Galatia.

Jude Brief letter warning against false teachers, used by the writer of II Peter (perhaps the same person); it may have been written in the 60s, but is more commonly dated in the 80s.

Judean Source Occasional, alternative name for J (q.v.).

Judges (Jg.) Chs. 1–3.6, introductions revealing the severe limits of the conquest under Joshua; 3.7–16, the history and exploits of the various judges; 17–18 first appendix on the migration of the Danites; 19–21, second on the sins of the Benjaminites. The victory (c. 1125 BC) of Barak and Deborah, chs. 4–5, marks the mid-point of the period.

Judith (Jdt.) The dramatic story of how the beautiful widow Judith saved her town from destruction by beguiling and then beheading the evil general Holofernes. Probably written in Hebrew in the 2nd cent. BC, perhaps as a more powerful and robust version of the theme of Esther.

Jung Codex Codex I from the Nag Hammadi library, taken to Zurich but now in Cairo, containing four books, including the Apocryphal Letter of JAMES and the Gospel of TRUTH.

jus primogeniturae (Latin) Rights of the first-born.

jus relictae (Latin) Rights of the widow.

jussive In Hebrew, the third person equivalent of an imperative, 'Let him . . .'.

K Hypothetical KENITE source within the Pentateuch that dealt with the life of Moses. (J. Morgenstern)

Kabbalah Later Jewish system of esoteric, mystical theology, whose origins derive from apocalyptic and Gnostic thought.

Kaddish (Aramaic) 'Holy'. Doxology of praise used in Jewish worship.

Kaige Recension Greek version of the OT from the 1st cent. AD or earlier, either a direct translation from the

Hebrew, or a revision of the SEPTUAGINT. Close to the version of THEODOTION, it is sometimes referred to as *Proto-Theodotion*.

kairos Greek for 'period of time', used to refer to the appointed time in the purposes of God, the time of crisis.

kapporeth (Hebrew) 'Mercy-seat', the cover of the Ark, where God's atoning mercy is shown. (Greek: HILASTERION)

katabasis (Greek) 'Descent', especially of Christ into Hades.

Kenite hypothesis Theory that YHWH was the mountain god of the Kenites, a Midianite clan in the Sinai wilderness, and that Moses first encountered him through his marriage to the daughter of Jethro the priest.

kenosis (Greek) 'Abasement', 'emptying'. The self-limiting of the Deity, particularly of the condescension involved in the Incarnation of the Son of God.

Keret, Legend of King Ugaritic text of the 14th cent. BC from RAS SHAMRA, a royal legend with a possible kernel of historical fact.

kerygma (Greek) 'Preaching'. The element of proclamation in the preaching of the Christian message, the good news, the gospel itself. Often distinguished from DIDACHE.

Kerygma Petrou Early 2nd cent. compilation of apostolic preaching. Known only from quotations, it was well regarded especially in Egypt until rejected as apocryphal. Not to be confused with KERYGMATA PETROU.

Kerygmata Petrou One of the earlier texts of the PSEUDO-CLEMENTINE literature, *c.* 200, from an anti-Pauline group of Jewish-Christians in Syria. It includes the *Epistula Petri* and *Contestatio*, and proclaims Jesus as the 'true Prophet' who fulfils the Law of Moses. Not to be confused with KERYGMA PETROU.

kerygmatic exegesis Occasional name for the approach that seeks to understand a biblical text in terms of the central confession of faith of its author or compiler; e.g. G. von Rad's assertion that the credal formula of Deut. 26.5b−9 provides the key to the whole Pentateuch.

kethibh (Hebrew) 'What is written'. A word written in the MASSORETIC TEXT of the Hebrew Bible, that is given a corrected reading (QERE) in the margin.

Ketubim or **Kethuvim** (Hebrew) 'Writings'. Title of the third section of the OT in the Hebrew canon, after the Torah and Nebiim. Also known to Christians as the *Hagiographa*.

khirbet (Arabic) 'Ruin'.

Khirbet Qumran Name of the archaeological site of the Qumran community and source of the DEAD SEA SCROLLS.

Kiddush (Hebrew) 'Sanctification'. Prayer recited over a cup of wine before the first meal to consecrate the Sabbath or festival.

Kings, I (I Kg.) Chs. 1–2, the conclusion of the SUCCESSION NARRATIVE; 3–11, the reign of Solomon; 12–22, the kings of Israel and Judah down to *c.* 850 BC, and including the ELIJAH CYCLE.

Kings, II (II Kg.) Originally part of a single book with I Kings. Chs. 1–17, the kings of Israel and Judah from *c.* 850 BC to the fall of the Northern Kingdom in 721 BC, and including the ELISHA CYCLE; 18–25, the last kings of Judah, down to the fall of Jerusalem in 587 BC, and including the ISAIAH SOURCE.

Kings of Israel, Annals of the and **Kings of Judah, Annals of the** Lost royal archives referred to by the Deuteronomic Historian.

kinsha Samaritan equivalent of the synagogue.

Klage (German) 'Lament', 'complaint', 'dirge'.

ko-amar formula 'Thus says . . .': the messenger formula which legitimizes the speaker and compels the hearer to accept the words coming from the sender, usually someone of higher rank. It is the classic opening formula of the prophetic oracles, in the form 'Thus says the LORD'.

Koine (Greek) The 'common' Greek of the eastern Mediterranean that followed the conquests of Alexander the Great, in which the NT was written. It is sometimes subdivided, though not very precisely, as follows:

Hellenistic Greek for the last three centuries BC.

NT Greek for the Christian writings of the first two centuries AD.

Patristic Greek for the Christian writings from the 3rd to the 8th cent. AD.

Koine Text Another name for the BYZANTINE, or LUCIANIC, TEXT.

koinonia (Greek) 'Communion', 'fellowship'.

Kompositionsgeschichte (German) 'Composition history'. Uncommon synonym for REDAKTIONSGESCHICHTE.

Korahite Psalms Pss. 42–9; 84–9. Two collections of Psalms, ascribed to the (post-exilic) sons of Korah, the first of which was included in the ELOHIST PSALTER, the second appended to it.

krisis (Greek) 'Judgement', usually of God.

Kultgeschichtliche Schule (German) 'Cult-History School'. Former offshoot of the form critical approach that laid stress on the religious cult rather than the literary form as the main formative influence on the transmission and development of the tradition.

Kunstspruch (German) 'Artistic saying'. An aphorism coming from a professional sage as opposed to a popular proverb (VOLKSSPRUCH); the book of Proverbs written by the Jerusalem school of sages naturally falls into this category.

Kyrios (Greek) 'Lord'. The Septuagint translation of the Hebrew ADONAI, and thus the pronounceable substitute for the unpronounceable YHWH. In the NT it also refers to Jesus Christ.

L (1) (NT) The material on the life and teaching of Jesus (but not the infancy narrative) found only in Luke's Gospel, sometimes reckoned to be an earlier document, sometimes as written by Luke himself. (B. Streeter)

(2) (OT) Hypothetical *Lay Source* (German: *Laienschrift*), older even than J, within the Pentateuch. So called because it contrasted strongly with the later Priestly Source. (O. Eissfeldt)

Lachish Letters Some 18 ostraca in Hebrew, not all of which are decipherable, sent by the commander of an outpost to his superior in the city itself, just before it was besieged by the Babylonians in 589 BC.

lacuna Gap or missing part of a manuscript.

Lake Group Group of NT MINUSCULES, from the 12th to 14th cent., that go back to the CAESAREAN TEXT.

Lamentations (Lam.) Five laments upon Jerusalem, destroyed by the Babylonians in 587 BC, written as ACROSTICS in the QINAH METRE. Composed in Palestine during the period of the Exile, undoubtedly not by Jeremiah, they give a powerful picture of the horror and despair of the ruined city and ravaged country.

language event Term derived from the philosophical understanding that reality and language are inseparable, that reality becomes such, for us as men, only as it is expressed in language. Thus the NT is/expresses the reality/language event of the Word made flesh; or put another way, it is the witness to the becoming real/the *language gain* of the Word made flesh.

langue (French) 'Tongue', 'language'. In structural analysis, the abstract, social language-system, as opposed to *parole*, the individual utterance.

Laodiceans, Epistle to the Brief and worthless forgery, made sometime between the 2nd and 4th cent., a pastiche of passages from Paul's epistles, in particular Philippians, based on a suggestion in Col. 4.16.

lapidary script Style of letters used on monuments or other stone surfaces, as opposed to that used on clay or papyrus.

lapsus calami (Latin) 'Slip of the pen'.

Lasterkatalog (German) 'Catalogue of vices'; a literary device used in ethical teaching of the NT period; e.g. Gal. 5.19f. Sometimes with as many as 22 items (the number of letters in the Hebrew alphabet), e.g. Rom. 1.29–31 or Didache 5.1, they may derive from hellenistic Jewish sources. Opposite of a TUGENDKATALOG.

latreia (Greek) The supreme worship and service due to God alone.

laxism Pejorative term for the relaxation of the moral or ritual obligations of the faith.

Leben-Jesu Forschung (German) 'Lives of Jesus research'. The recreation and analysis of a historical biography.

lectio difficilior (Latin) The more difficult, grammatically or theologically, of two or more readings in the manuscripts of a text; often regarded as more likely to be original for that reason.

lectio marginalis (Latin) 'Reading in the margin'.

Lectionaries In textual criticism, the service books of the Greek-speaking Church, dating from the 7th cent. onwards, which give a reading from the Gospel and another from the Epistles (including Acts but not Revelation) for each day of the year.

lehrhafte Darstellungen (German) 'Didactic expositions'. Technical term suggesting an oral and literary form for the summaries of history and faith in the early OT.

lemma Sub-title giving the substance of the following text.

levirate marriage Mosaic regulation whereby if a man dies leaving his widow childless, his surviving brother must marry her to give him descendants, Deut. 25.5ff.

Leviticus (Lev.) Large section of laws from the PRIESTLY source: chs. 1–7, on sacrifice; 8–10, consecration of priests; 11–15, clean and unclean; 16, the Day of Atonement; 17–26, the HOLINESS CODE; 27, religious vows.

lexeme An individual word or word stem.

lex talionis (Latin) 'The law of retaliation' – Ex. 21.23f, 'An eye for an eye, a tooth for a tooth, . . .'.

liberation theology Recent theological movement, active in Latin America and usually involving a Marxist analysis, that sees Christianity not in terms of individual salvation but of liberation of a people from their oppression, after the model of the Exodus, when God led his people out of bondage in Egypt.

Life of Jesus theology Theology based on the belief that the results of the Life of Jesus research, the recreation of a historical biography, are fundamental and normative for Christian faith.

lingua franca Common, international language, such as Latin in the Middle Ages or Akkadian in the ancient Near East.

lingua sacra Sacred language used only in a religious context, such as Hebrew among the Jews after it had been superseded by Aramaic as the everyday language.

litotes The emphatic use of understatement, by employing a negative; e.g. Acts 21.39, 'a citizen of no mean city'.

locus classicus (Latin) The key passage in the Bible most often quoted to explain or support an idea or doctrine; e.g. Heb. 9.25ff for the completeness of Christ's sacrifice.

logion (Greek) 'Saying'. Used mainly in the plural, *logia*, to refer to the sayings of Jesus.

95

logogram Sign or character representing a complete word.

Logoi Sophon (Greek) 'Words of the Wise'. Suggested literary genre of late OT Wisdom teaching, based on the SAYINGS OF THE WISE section of Proverbs, and itself the basis of early Christian sayings collections such as Q, M, L and the forerunner of the Gospel of THOMAS.

Logos theology or **Logos Christology** Teaching or apologetic that lays stress on Jesus as the Logos, the Word of God, Jn. 1.1.

LORD See YHWH.

lower criticism Former title, distinguished from HIGHER CRITICISM, and now rarely used, for what is in effect TEXTUAL CRITICISM.

Lucianic Text Text of the Greek Bible revised by Lucian of Antioch (d. 312), which soon became standard and the basis of the BYZANTINE TEXT. Also known as the *Antiochene Text* or the *Syrian Text*.

Luke (Lk.) With Acts, part of a longer, literary work in good Greek by a Gentile Christian, commonly reckoned to have used Mark, Q and L as sources; written some time between the late 60s and late 80s, much the same period as Matthew.

Luke's Great Omission That major section of Mark, 6.45–8.26, that has no parallel in Luke.

LXX Common abbreviation for the SEPTUAGINT.

M The material on the life and teaching of Jesus (but not the infancy narrative) found only in Matthew's Gospel, sometimes reckoned to be an earlier document, sometimes as written by Matthew himself. (B. Streeter)

maat (Egyptian) 'Order', 'justice', based around the person of the Pharoah.

macarism Synonym, from the Greek, for 'beatitude', an accounting happy.

Maccabees, Books of Four Jewish works all by different writers; none are in the Hebrew canon, the first two in the Latin canon, all four in the Greek.

I The most valuable of the four, it is the main historical source for the Maccabean period, from 175 to 134 BC at which point the book ends; written in Hebrew by a Jew of Jerusalem some time before the end of the century.

II An abridgement of a work by Jason of Cyrene covering the period of the Maccabean revolt. It often supplements the information in the first book, but is generally of less historical value, showing rather a love of the miraculous and containing a eulogy of martyrdom; in Greek, early 1st cent. BC.

III A turgid account of Ptolemy IV's attempted entry into the Temple in 217 BC and his persecution of Jews in Egypt and their miraculous deliverance by angels; in Greek at the end of the 1st cent. BC, in Alexandria.

IV A philosophical diatribe on the superiority of devout reason over passion; in Greek, before AD 70, in Alexandria.

magi (Greek) 'Wise men', 'masters of the secret, astrological arts', among whom the three wise men of Mt. 2.2. Some 2nd cent. Christian sects saw Jesus as the greatest of the magi.

magnalia Dei (Latin) 'The mighty acts of God'.

Magnificat Lk. 1.46–55. The Song of Mary.

Major Prophets Isaiah, Jeremiah, Ezekiel.

majuscule Script written in large or capital letters, as contrasted with minuscule or cursive script.

Malachi (Mal.) A CULT PROPHET of perhaps the 5th cent. BC who condemned the laxity of worship in Jerusalem, and prophesied a forerunner, that a concluding addition identifies as Elijah, to prepare for the coming day of judgement.

Manasseh, Prayer of Penitential prayer seemingly based upon II Chron. 33.12f, included as a short book of the Apocrypha; its date and original language are both uncertain.

Mandates of Hermas See HERMAS, SHEPHERD OF.

Manichaeism Sect founded by Manes, a 3rd cent. Persian, influenced by Gnosticism and Zoroastrianism and influencing many Christians, characterized by a very strict dualism between Good and Evil, which encouraged extreme asceticism.

Manual of Discipline Another name for the COMMUNITY RULE.

Maranatha Early Christian invocation in Aramaic, 'O Lord come!' or 'The Lord is come!'; I Cor. 16.22.

Märchen   (German) 'Fairy tales', 'folk tales'.

Marcion, Gospel of   Marcion's edited version of the Gospel of Luke, which with ten letters of Paul, made up his CANON of Scripture.

Marcionite   Relating to the 2nd cent. heretic Marcion, who rejected the OT and its law as incompatible with the gospel message of the NT, and devised his own canon of scripture. The term is sometimes used for any Christian who rejects or undervalues the OT.

Marcionite Prologues   Short introductions to the Pauline epistles, written by Marcionites in Rome, late 2nd cent., and found in many manuscripts of the Vulgate.

Mariology   That part of theology dealing with the person and importance of the Blessed Virgin Mary.

Mari Texts   Some 20,000 cuneiform tablets, mainly in Akkadian from the 18th cent. BC, on economic, political and administrative matters, from the Mari Empire on the upper Euphrates.

Mark   (Mk.) Generally reckoned to have been the earliest of the gospels; early 60s, written perhaps from Rome, traditionally from the teaching of Peter.

Mark, Secret Gospel of   An 18th cent. Greek manuscript discovered in 1958 records part of letter by Clement of Alexandria, which speaks of a 'secret gospel' of Mark, quoting an addition to Mk. 10 that reveals Jésus giving secret teaching to certain disciples by night. It suggests an esoteric expansion to the Gospel, made in Alexandria in the 2nd cent.

mashal   (Hebrew) 'Proverb', 'maxim'; also a song or poem.

massorah   (Hebrew) 'Tradition'. Signs and notes for text-critical and exegetical clarification, corrected readings and instructions to copyists, added to the MASSORETIC TEXT.

Massoretic Text   (MT) The definitive text of the Hebrew Bible. Drawn up by Jewish scholars known as the *Massoretes*, between the 6th and the 10th cent., it included vowel pointing and notes around the basic consonantal text.

matres lectionis   Consonants used to represent vowel sounds, where no proper vowels exist in that script; e.g. *yodh* and *waw* in Hebrew.

Matthew   (Mt.) Commonly reckoned to have made use of

Mark, with the addition of sayings collections Q and M, though the hypothesis of an Aramaic original, or that it is the earliest of the Synoptics, is occasionally revived; written some time from the late 60s to the late 80s by a Jewish Christian, probably near Antioch.

mea culpa (Latin) 'Through my fault'. An expression of confession or culpability.

Megilloth (Hebrew) 'Rolls'. Name for five shorter books of the KETUBIM, which were read out at festivals: Ruth, Song of Solomon, Ecclesiastes, Lamentations and Esther.

meiosis (Greek) 'Lessening'. The literary or rhetorical use of understatement.

memoria technica (Latin) System or technique used to aid one's memory.

Memphitic Earlier and misleading name for the BOHAIRIC dialect of Coptic.

memra (Hebrew) 'Word'; used in late OT Judaism for the creative word of God, or as a circumlocution for the divine name.

Menologion A LECTIONARY for the fixed, ecclesiastical year.

messianic secret Major literary theme in Mark's Gospel in particular, where Jesus explicitly enjoins secrecy on all who perceive his messianic status, until right at the end at his trial (14.62).

messianism Belief in a coming Messiah.

metalanguage Language about language.

metanoia (Greek) 'Repentance', 'conversion'.

metaphrase A slavishly literal translation.

metaphysics That branch of philosophy that deals with ultimate abstract principles, such as space, time, being, reality and so on.

metempsychosis Migration of the soul from one body to another until purification is achieved, i.e. reincarnation.

methodology The science of method; the analysis of one's method of analysis.

metonymy Figure of speech in which a word is used to refer to something greater associated with it, most often a concrete object for an abstract, such as 'sword' for 'war' or 'sceptre' for 'authority'.

Micah (Mic.) A younger contemporary of First Isaiah from a village south of Jerusalem, who began preaching *c.* 730 BC. His prophecies of the total destruction of the city and the complete renewal of the Davidic dynasty in the first part of the book became the basis for a post-exilic prophecy of restoration in the second part.

Michaeas Latin form of MICAH.

midrash (Hebrew) Interpretation of Scripture. More specifically a Jewish homiletic commentary on a biblical text, of the late OT period onwards, often with added allegory and legends.

millenarianism or **millenianism** Belief and hope, inspired by the apocalyptic literature, in the imminent second coming of Christ, and his thousand year rule on earth.

mimesis (Greek) 'Imitation'. The ability of literature to imitate real life; or of a figure of speech in which the words or actions of another are imitated.

Minor Prophets The twelve shorter prophetic works, Hosea–Malachi.

minuscules Greek manuscripts of the Bible written in small, joined letters (cursive script); they superseded UNCIALS from the 8th cent.

miqra' sopherim (Hebrew) 'Pronounciation of the scribes'. Accepted way of reading certain words in the consonantal text of the Hebrew Bible, from before the invention of VOWEL POINTS.

Mischungen (German) 'Mixed forms'.

misharum (Akkadian) 'Justice', 'equity'.

Mishnah (Hebrew) 'Study', 'repetition'. Collection of oral traditions and exegesis of the Jewish Scribes and Rabbis, almost entirely legal in content (HALAKHAH). Written in Hebrew, its compilation was attributed to Rabbi Judah in the second half of the 2nd cent. AD. Divided into six sections it forms the basis of the TALMUD.

mishpat (Hebrew) 'Judgement', 'justice'.

Mithraism Cult of Mithras, a Persian sun god, that spread to Rome soon after Christianity. Popular with the army, it had a sacramental system not dissimilar to that of the Church, though any influence is improbable.

Moabite Stone Inscription in Moabite, a language similar to Hebrew, *c.* 850 BC, recounting a victory over Israel, whose own version of the battle occurs in II Kg. 3.

Modernism   Roman Catholic movement at the beginning of this century that sought to make room for biblical criticism and liberal philosophy within the teaching of the Church.

modus operandi   (Latin) 'Mode of operation', way of doing things.

modus vivendi   (Latin) 'Mode of living'; an arrangement of peaceful co-existence between antagonists.

monachism   Used for *monasticism* in its early development.

Monarchian Prologues   Short 4th cent. introductions to the four gospels in rather obscure Latin, describing the evangelists and their purpose in writing, found in many manuscripts of the Vulgate.

monogeny   Belief in the origin of mankind from one common pair, Adam and Eve.

monograph   Detailed study of a specific subject, as opposed to a general survey or introduction.

monolatry   Worship of only one God. In practice often synonymous with HENOTHEISM.

monotheism   Belief in, and exclusive worship of, one God. Often distinguished further:

primitive monotheism   The original, earliest religious impulse of man, to believe in a single transcendent being.

militant monotheism   Belief in one God, and the proclamation of this faith in a society where other gods are professed; e.g. Elijah on Mount Carmel, I Kg. 18.

strict (or **philosophical**) **monotheism**   Belief in one God without conceiving the logical possibility that any other god could exist. Deutero-Isaiah is reckoned to be the first and grandest exponent.

ethical monotheism   There is only one God, and his existence demands our obedience. Ascribed either to Deutero-Isaiah alone, or to the whole prophetic movement from Elijah onwards.

Montanism   Apocalyptic movement of the latter half of the 2nd cent., derived from Montanus of Phrygia. Enthusiastic and ascetic, it sought the imminent outpouring of the Holy Spirit on the Church.

Moreh Zedek Hebrew for the TEACHER OF RIGHTEOUSNESS.
morpheme The smallest unit of meaning in the structure of a language; e.g. the word 'atonement' is made up of three morphemes, at, one and -ment.
Moses, Apocalypse of Misleading name for the shorter recension of the Book of ADAM AND EVE.
Moses, Assumption of Jewish apocalyptic work written in the 1st cent. BC and revised in the 1st cent AD, in either Hebrew or Aramaic; only a testament of Moses to Joshua remains, reworking the last chapters of Deuteronomy.
Moses, Testament of Alternative name for the Assumption of MOSES.
ms/mss Common abbreviation for manuscript/manuscripts.
MT Common abbreviation for the MASSORETIC TEXT.
Murabba'at Texts Letters from Simon bar Kochba, leader of the Second Jewish Revolt (132–5), and contemporary biblical texts that give evidence of the PROTO-MASSORETIC TEXT.
Murashu Tablets Some 730 cuneiform tablets of the second half of the 5th cent. BC. from the business house of the Murashu family in Nippur, giving evidence of the presence and activity of Jews in Babylonia.
Muratorian Canon Earliest catalogue of the books of the NT, late 2nd cent. and written in very bad Latin; its list differs somewhat from the present canon.
mutatis mutandis (Latin) With due alteration of details.
mystagogy Preparatory instruction for initiation into a MYSTERY CULT.
mysterion (Greek) 'Mystery', usually a religious mystery, and in Christian writings invariably the gospel itself.
mysterium tremendum The awful mystery, the numinous power of God.
mystery cult Form of religion particularly popular in the Hellenistic world and with possible influence on early Christianity; characterized by a long, complex initiation that granted the worshipper the secret that would free him from the world of suffering and gain him a share in the immortality of the god he worships.
mytheme In structural analysis, a component in the structure of a myth.

mythogony Study of the origin of myths.
mythopoeic Relating to the making of myths.

Nabatean (Aramaic) Dialect of the turn of the era, found on inscriptions to the south-east of Palestine.
nabi (Hebrew) 'Prophet'. (Plural: NEBIIM)
Nabonidus Chronicle Babylonian text, probably written in the time of Cyrus his conqueror, that records the last years of Nabonidus, king of Babylon (556–539 BC).
Nachgeschichte (German) History of the 'after-life' of an early text, within the biblical tradition.
Nag Hammadi Papyri Collection of about fifty works, contained in thirteen complete or partial codices, written in Coptic in the 4th cent., which were discovered in Egypt in 1945. They appear to be the contents of a library, perhaps belonging to Chenoboskion a nearby monastic centre; most are Gnostic writings and many were previously unknown, the most significant being the Gospel of THOMAS. They now carry the siglum CG (Cairensis Gnosticus); some other similar works discovered in 1896 are included in the collection under the siglum BG (Berolinensis Gnosticus).
Nahum (Nah.) Oracle of judgement on the Assyrian city of Nineveh, shortly before it fell in 612 BC.
Nash Papyrus Small Hebrew fragment of the 2nd cent. BC, containing the DECALOGUE and the SHEMA.
natural theology That understanding of God and the divine order that can be gained by man's reason without the aid of revelation.
Naturweisheit (German) 'Knowledge of nature'; one of the goals of the WISDOM tradition.
Nazarenes, Gospel of the See HEBREWS, GOSPEL OF THE.
Nebiim (Hebrew) 'Prophets'. Title of the second of the three sections of the Hebrew Bible.
necromancy Communication with the dead; e.g. Saul and the Witch of Endor, I Sam. 28.3ff.
Nehemiah (Neh.) Part of the larger work of the CHRONI-CLER. Nehemiah is generally reckoned to have returned to Jerusalem as governor twice in the reign of Artaxerxes I (464–423 BC) and rebuilt the walls of the city; he therefore

came *before* Ezra. The text is severely disrupted; for a reconstruction, see EZRA.

neo-creationism See CREATIONISM.

neophyte New convert; I Tim, 3.6.

Neo-Platonism Revival of Plato's philosophy, from the 3rd to the 6th cent. AD, that sought to establish a firm intellectual basis for the moral and religious life. With a strong mystical emphasis, on the priority of the transcendent 'One' over the many, it had a considerable influence upon Christianity.

Neutral Text More commonly known nowadays as the ALEXANDRIAN TEXT.

Nicodemus, Gospel of Later name given to two 4th cent. texts, the Acts of PILATE and the DESCENT INTO HELL, that were combined in the 5th cent.

Noah, Apocalypse of Better known as the Book of NOAH.

Noah, Book of Incorporated into I ENOCH, 6–11; 54.7–55.2; 60; 65–69.25; 106–7, and into the Book of JUBILEES, it describes the fall of the angels and the corruption of men as the cause of the Flood, working from Gen. 6.1ff, and the marvellous birth of Noah; probably in Aramaic, early 2nd cent. BC.

nomadism The wandering, nomadic way of life, characteristic of Israel's ancestors, often described more precisely as

    semi-nomadism where the clan travels with its flocks for only part of the year and practices some form of simple agriculture; or

    enclosed nomadism where those who wander do so within the geographical confines of a settled society, with which they interact.

nomina sacra (Latin) 'Sacred names'. Early Christian scribal practice of contracting the words 'God', 'Lord', 'Jesus' and 'Christ' and placing a line above, out of reverence for their holiness.

nomothetic Name given to the so-called 'new archeology' approach that seeks a more generalized, over-all explanation of the past than was previously sought.

nous (Greek) 'Mind', 'the faculty of thought'.

Novelle (German) 'Short story'; used by some scholars in preference to 'saga' in various biblical contexts.

104

NT New Testament.

Numbers (Num.) 1.1–10.10, census and preparations to leave Sinai; 10.11–20.13, journey to Kadesh and an unsuccessful attack on Canaan; 20.14–36.13, journey to the east of the Jordan. Mostly from the PRIESTLY source, with older traditions particularly in the third section, it recounts Israel's time in the wilderness.

numen (Adjective: *numinous*) Divine power or presence; has the sense of awe and self-abasement in the face of utter holiness; particularly characteristic of the early OT.

Nunc Dimittis Lk. 2.29–32. The Song of Simeon.

Nuzi Texts Several thousand cuneiform tablets of Hurrian archives, written in Akkadian in the mid-2nd millenium BC, when Nuzi was a provincial city of the Mitanni Empire, throwing light on the legal and cultural background of the partriarchal age and the major source on the HABIRU.

ob. (Latin: *obiit*) 'He died'; usually followed by a date.

Obadiah (Ob.) Short oracle of judgement upon the Edomites, from the early years of the Exile; vv. 1–9 are paralleled in Jer. 49.7–22.

obiter dictum (Latin) '(Something) said by the way'; an incidental remark.

Occam's Razor The philosophical principle that beings and theories should not be multiplied unnecessarily, that urges simplicity in logic and explanation.

Octateuch Name for the first eight books of the OT, Genesis–Ruth.

odium theologicum (Modern Latin) Hatred and bitter rivalry characteristic of theological disputes.

oikonomia (Greek) 'Management'. God's plan of salvation for the world.

oikoumene (Greek) 'The inhabited world'.

Old Greek Version Name given to the earliest form of the SEPTUAGINT text to distinguish it from the later LUCIANIC revision of the early 4th cent. AD. Also known as the *Proto-Septuagint*.

Old Latin Versions (Vet. Lat.) Latin translations of the Bible prior to the VULGATE. Also known as the *Itala*.

Old Syriac Version   Syriac translation of the NT prior to the PESHITTA.

omphalos   (Greek) 'Navel'. The centre point of the earth.

onomasticon   List or classification of names, either as an aid to their meaning and etymology, or as a classification of natural phenomena in later Wisdom literature; e.g. Wis. 7.17ff.

onomatopoeia   (Hebrew poetry) Rhetorical device in which words are used that sound like what they describe.

ontology   That part of philosophy that deals with being and existence.

op. cit.   (Latin) The book or text already cited.

opisthograph   Text written on the VERSO of a roll already used for some other purpose.

orthography   Spelling and its rules and conventions.

orthopraxy   The observance of correct religious actions and practice; as distinct from the adherence to correct doctrines, which is *orthodoxy*.

Ortsgebundenheit   (German) The attachment and development of a tradition around a local shrine, in the early OT period.

Osee   Latin form of HOSEA.

ossuary   Urn containing bones of the dead.

ostracon   (Greek for 'potsherd'). Piece of pottery used for a short written text such as a letter or memorandum; quite common throughout the ancient world.

OT   Old Testament.

ousia   (Greek) 'Being', 'essence', 'substance'.

oxymoron   (Greek) 'Pointedly foolish'. Rhetorical juxtaposition of contradictory terms; e.g. 'living water', Jn. 4.10.

Oxyrhynchus Papyri   Several thousand papyrus fragments discovered at Oxyrhynchus in Upper Egypt. Dating from the 2nd cent. BC. to the 7th AD and in several languages, some of the most important are the following, in Greek:

P. Ox. 1, 654, 655   Sayings of Jesus similar to those in the Gospel of THOMAS; 2nd or 3rd cent.

P. Ox. 840   An otherwise unknown incident of Jesus and his disciples in the Jerusalem Temple and a dispute with a chief priest; copied in minute letters in the 4th cent.

P The *Priestly Source*: the last and most extensive of the four main sources of the Pentateuch. Written by priests in the 6th cent. BC and incorporating earlier traditions, it is characterized by a concern for ritual, long genealogies, the avoidance of anthropomorphism and a precise, ordered style. The whole of Leviticus, including the HOLINESS CODE, forms part of it.

pace (Latin) 'By leave of. . . .', written before naming someone who disagrees with the hypothesis that one is putting forward.

paedobaptism Baptism of infants.

pais (Greek) 'Servant', 'son'. Possibly an early title of Jesus, e.g. Didache 9.2.

palaeography Science or art of deciphering and dating ancient scripts and writing. Hence *palaeograph*, an ancient writing.

Palestinian Syriac Version Independent translation of the NT, probably 5th cent., into Christian Palestinian Aramaic.

palimpsest Manuscript that has been written on twice, the first text having been, often imperfectly, rubbed out. It is this older writing that is normally of most interest.

palingenesis (Greek) 'Rebirth', 'regeneration'.

palladium Something on which the safety of the nation depends; e.g. the Ark of the Covenant in the time of the Judges.

Palmyrene (Aramaic) Dialect of the early Christian centuries in the deserts of Syria and North Arabia.

panegyric Public speech of praise; a eulogy.

panegyris or **panegyry** Religious festival in praise of God.

panentheism Belief that God's Being is in every part of creation. Not to be confused with PANTHEISM.

pantheism Belief that God and the Universe are identical: God is everything and everything is God.

Papias Bishop of Hierapolis in the early 2nd cent. he collected oral traditions concerning the Apostles. Though of questionable reliability and known only in quotation, they are often included among the APOSTOLIC FATHERS.

papponymy Taking one's name from one's grandfather.

parablepsis (Greek) 'Looking to the side'. Copying error caused by the scribe's eye returning to the wrong line in the

107

text, easy enough if two adjacent lines begin or end with the same word.

paraclesis (Greek) 'Encouragement', 'consolation'.

Paraclete (Greek) 'Advocate', 'helper', 'comforter'. Title of the Holy Spirit, e.g. Jn. 14.16.

paradigm (Greek) 'Model', 'example'. Also used in a technical sense to refer to passages in the gospels which consist of a narrative woven around a saying of Jesus; e.g. the healing of the paralytic, Mk. 2.1–12. It is therefore much the same as an APOPHTHEGM or a PRONOUNCEMENT STORY.

paradigmatic relations The vertical, associative, synchronic relations within a text; the relations a word has with other words and ideas outside that particular text; as opposed to the SYNTAGMATIC RELATIONS.

paradosis (Greek) 'Tradition', that which is handed over.

paraenesis (Greek) 'Exhortation', 'encouragement', often of preaching in general.

Paralipomenon Greek name for the two books of CHRONICLES.

parallelismus membrorum (Latin) 'Parallelism of members'. The characteristic parallelism of Hebrew poetry, found in three main types:

synonymous parallelism where the second line of the couplet repeats the thought of the first.

antithetic parallelism where the second line is in contrast to the thought of the first.

synthetic parallelism where the theme of the first line is continued and developed in the second.

To these may be added:

step parallelism involving the use of ANADIPLOSIS.

chiastic parallelism involving the use of CHIASMUS.

parabolic parallelism involving the use of simile, 'As . . .: so . . .'.

parataxis Characteristic of Semitic writing in which the clauses are added one to another by 'and', with no indication of their precise syntactical relation.

pari passu (Latin) Simultaneously; side by side.

parole (French) 'Word', 'speech'. In structural analysis, the concrete, individual utterance, as opposed to *langue*, the abstract language-system.

108

paronomasia (Hebrew poetry) Punning, play on words; e.g. Is. 5.7, 'He looked for justice (mishpat) but behold bloodshed (mishpah); for righteousness (sedhaqa) but behold a cry (se'aqa).'

parousia (Greek) 'Coming', 'advent'; the second coming of Christ in glory to judge the world and redeem the faithful.

parthenogenesis (Greek) 'Virgin birth'. More appropriate in the field of biology than for the Blessed Virgin Mary and the birth of Jesus.

passim (Latin) Of a book cited, that the subject in question occurs here and there throughout its pages.

passional Narrative of the sufferings of saints and martyrs, read out at worship on their feast-day.

passion narrative Within each of the gospels, that final section that recounts the suffering and death of Jesus. It is possible that such narratives, most notably Mark's (chs. 14–16), existed as independent texts before the formation of the gospels.

Passover Haggadah Jewish collection of psalms, prayers and stories woven around the account of the Exodus, for use at the annual Passover meal. Compiled much later from the Bible, Mishnah and midrash, it may however reflect some traditions of the 1st cent. AD.

Pastoral Epistles Common title for I & II Timothy and Titus.

pathetic fallacy Misleadingly derogatory title for the figure of speech that ascribes human characteristics to inanimate objects; e.g. 'Let the heavens be glad: let the earth rejoice', Ps. 96.11.

pathetic history Historical narrative that seeks to entertain the reader by playing on his emotions, with tales of horrors and heroism, of terrible dangers and sudden miracles; II & III Maccabees.

Patriarchal Age 2000–1500 BC, during the Middle Bronze Age, the Patriarchs being Abraham, Isaac and Jacob.

patristics That branch of theology that studies the writings of the early Fathers of the Church, the theologians from the end of the 1st cent. to about the 8th.

patrology A systematically arranged manual on the patristic writings.

Paul, Acts of Unusual among the 2nd cent. apocryphal Acts in that it was written by an orthodox Christian, in Greek in Asia Minor. It contains the *Acts of Paul and Thecla*, which may contain some historical truth including a description of Paul's physical appearance, the 3rd Epistle to the CORINTHIANS and the *Martyrdom of Paul*.

Paul, Apocalypse of Greek apocryphon of the late 4th cent. probably by a monk, giving a detailed description of Paul's visions when he was 'caught up to the third heaven' (II Cor. 12.2).

Pearl, Hymn of the Beautiful Gnostic poem that describes the deliverance of the soul as the gaining of the 'one pearl', found in the Acts of THOMAS (sections 108–13).

pedilavium (Latin) 'Washing of feet'; Jn. 13.

peirasmos (Greek) 'Temptation'.

Pentateuch Genesis–Deuteronomy. The five books of Moses; the books of the Law; the Torah.

Perfection, Gospel of A Gnostic treatise known only from a reference in Epiphanius.

performative utterances Those occasions of speech where the descriptive content of the language is secondary to its function of exciting certain emotions or behaviour. The liturgy is full of examples, e.g. the response 'The Lord be with you: and also with you'.

peribole Enclosure, usually walled, around a temple or sanctuary.

pericope Short portion of Scripture, most often of the gospels, forming a self-contained literary unit.

Pericope Adulterae Jn. 7.53–8.11. Story of the woman caught in adultery; not found in the earliest manuscripts of the Gospel.

peripeteia (Greek) 'Sudden change'. A dramatic turn of events in a narrative, such as Nathan's 'Thou art the man!', II Sam. 12.7.

periphrasis The use of more words than necessary to express one's meaning, whether as a deliberate figure of speech or through literary incompetence.

peristyle Colonnade surrounding a temple.

pesher (Hebrew) 'Interpretation'. Technical term for the type of biblical commentary found at Qumran.

Peshitta The official translation of the Bible for Syriac-speaking Christians; from the early 5th cent.

Peter, I (I Pet.) One of the Catholic Epistles; sent to encourage Christians in Asia Minor. Written in good Greek, probably by Silvanus (5.12) on behalf of Peter, from Rome *c.* 64.

Peter, II (II Pet.) Clearly written by a different hand to that of the first letter, it may be an expansion of Jude. Generally dated the last of the NT works, even as late as 150.

Peter, Acts of One of the late 2nd cent. Greek apocryphal Acts, it shows the encratite and docetic tendencies common to popular literature of the time. It includes a contest with Simon Magus, which was later developed in the PSEUDO-CLEMENTINES, and a *Martyrdom*.

Peter, Apocalypse of Written early in the 2nd cent., it is the most important of the apocryphal Christian apocalypses; extant in two recensions, Ethiopic and Akhmimic, it gives detailed descriptions of heaven and hell.

Peter, Gospel of Early 2nd cent. Greek apocryphon of which only the passion narrative is extant; dependant on the canonical gospels it is anti-Jewish and docetic in character, but very restrained in comparison with later Gnostic gospels.

Peter, Martyrdom of Most important section of the Acts of PETER, often found on its own, recounting the QUO VADIS incident and his crucifixion upside down.

petitio ad misericordiam (Latin) 'Appeal to (usually God's) mercy'.

petitio principii (Latin) Begging the question; not dissimilar to a circular argument, in which the premise is as much in need of proof as the conclusion supposedly based upon it.

phatic communion Use of language to establish rapport rather than to convey information, notably in greetings.

phenomenology Literally 'the study of phenomena', more particularly the analysis and description of the essences and essential meanings inherent in the fundamental structure of our experience, without any recourse to metaphysics as a means of explanation. An approach characteristic of much European philosophy in the earlier part of this century.

Philemon (Phm.) Brief note from Paul sent to Philemon of Colossae, with Onesimus his runaway slave.

philia (Greek) 'Brotherly love', 'friendship'.

Philip, Gospel of Coptic text from Nag Hammadi, going back to a 2nd cent. original from Syria. A Valentinian Gnostic work, it consists of a series of loosely connected theological reflections, making free use of NT material.

Philippians (Phil.) Personal and joyful letter whose Pauline authorship is not in doubt; generally ascribed to the time of his captivity, early 60s.

philology Linguistics; the study of language.

philosophia perennis (Latin) The, generally Platonist, mainstream of Western philosophy over the last couple of thousand years.

philosophical theology That branch of theology that seeks to describe the central truths of the Christian faith in rational terms consistent with the contemporary philosophical understanding.

Philoxenian Version Syriac version of the NT made in 508, of which little evidence survives as it was superseded by the HARKLEAN VERSION.

Phoenician One of the north-western Semitic group of languages, spoken on the coastal plain from Tyre and Sidon to Byblos. The alphabet appears to have been invented here.

phoneme A phonetic unit; a speech sound, as classified in a language – consonants, vowels, semi-vowels, stresses, etc.

phonogram Written character representing a spoken sound or phoneme.

phonology Study of vocal sounds and their combination.

phusis (Greek) 'Nature', 'essence'.

pictograph A pictorial symbol, as in the very earliest form of writing.

pietism Properly a 17th cent. revival of piety and devotional prayer in the Lutheran Church; used generally as a pejorative term for a faith of exaggerated piety.

Pilate, Acts of Not, despite its name, one of the APOCRYPHAL ACTS, but an account of the trial of Jesus expanded from the material in the canonical gospels, possibly in reply to the anti-Christian trial narratives produced under Emperor Maximin; Greek, early 4th cent. It is now found with the DESCENT INTO HELL as the Gospel of NICODEMUS.

Pilgrimage Songs Title given to Pss. 120–34; short post-exilic psalms sung by pilgrims to Jerusalem. Also known as the *Songs of Ascents* or the *Songs of Degrees*.

Pirqe Aboth Collection of short sayings of some sixty of the early Rabbis, mostly moral in character, forming the oldest tractate of the MISHNAH; Hebrew and Aramaic, it was compiled between AD 70 and 170, but with an oral tradition going back much further.

Pistis Sophia Curious 3rd cent. Egyptian Gnostic apocryphon relating Christ's instructions to his disciples at the end of the twelve-year post-resurrection period.

pleonasm Superfluous or redundant expression; the use of more words than is necessary; e.g. Mk. 2.25 of David, 'when he was in need and was hungry'.

pleroma (Greek) 'Fulness', 'completeness', Col. 2.9; but particularly in Gnostic thought, the spiritual universe as the totality of God's power.

pneuma (Greek) 'Spirit'. (Hebrew: *ruah*)

pneumatic In Gnostic thought, that which is spiritual, as opposed to HYLIC, material.

pneumatikoi (Greek) 'Spirit-filled people', I Cor. 3.1. In Gnostic thought, the select few who have received the full GNOSIS.

pneumatology Branch of theology dealing with the Holy Spirit.

pneumatophany Grotesque technical term for an appearance of the Holy Spirit, as at Pentecost.

Poimandres Part of the HERMETIC LITERATURE.

poimenic Relating to pastoral theology and writing.

pointed text Hebrew text with VOWEL POINTS added.

Polycarp, Epistle of Letter to the Philippians written by Polycarp, bishop of Smyrna, early in the 2nd cent.; not to be confused with the letter *to* Polycarp from Ignatius, which is also included among the APOSTOLIC FATHERS. It asks about the recently martyred Ignatius and gives a pastoral warning about DOCETISM and GNOSTICISM, for us a major insight into the maintaining of orthodoxy in the Sub-Apostolic Church.

Polycarp, Martyrdom of Contemporary account of the trial and martyrdom of Polycarp, the 86 year old bishop of Smyrna, in 155, sent by the Church at Smyrna to Christians in Philomelium; included among the APOSTOLIC FATHERS.

113

polyglots Editions of the Bible containing several texts or translations in parallel columns, in particular those of the 16th and 17th cent. by Cardinal Ximenes at Toledo, and later from Antwerp, Paris and London.

polyphone Written character used to represent several sounds.

polysemy Multiplicity of meaning.

polysyndeton The use of several conjunctions close together, a characteristic of NT Greek.

polytheism Faith in, and worship of, several gods. Often used too freely, it is confused with *polydaemonism*, belief in a multiplicity of supernatural spirits. While the nature of a God tends to preclude more than one, so the nature of a spirit suggests that there must be several.

post-critical naïveté The deliberate return to a text as an ordinary reader once again, after one has finished submitting it to the full range of scholarly analysis.

post hoc (ergo) propter hoc (Latin) The error of confusing cause with mere temporal sequence.

praeparatio evangelica Something, usually a philosophical system, that provides a preparation for the understanding and acceptance of the gospel.

praxeis (Greek) 'Acts', especially of the APOCRYPHAL ACTS.

praxis (Greek, via Medieval Latin) 'Action', 'practice'. It means no more than that though the context often suggests as much.

presbyter (Greek) 'Elder'. Administrative leader of the synagogue or the early church.

preternatural Relating to that which surpasses the ordinary or natural.

prevenient grace Belief that the grace of God precedes the free choice of the human will; Rom. 8.29ff.

Priestly Source The fourth Pentateuchal source. See P.

prima facie (Latin) At first sight; on the face of it.

proairesis (Greek) 'Choice', 'faculty of free will'.

procatalepsis Literary style in which opponents' objections are answered in anticipation; a technique of Paul, e.g. Rom. 6.1.

process theology Contemporary theological movement which argues that God as supreme must be both unchangeable, which has always been asserted, *and* changing, i.e. that He himself is in the process of evolution through his intercourse with an evolving world. Rejecting the static quality of classical theism, it seeks to move closer to the biblical picture of a God who acts in history.

proclitic Monosyllable so unemphasized that its accent is pushed forward onto the following word.

proem Preface or prelude to a piece of writing. Also a less common name for the PROLOGUE of John.

prolegomena (Also, though rarer, in the singular *prolegomenon*) Preliminary study, or a detailed preamble to an area of study.

prolepsis Prophetic technique of treating a future event as past; e.g. Amos's funeral dirge on the fall of Israel, 5.1ff.

Prologue Unless otherwise qualified, the opening verses of John's Gospel, 1.1–18.

pronominal suffix One of ten Hebrew suffixes added to verbs, nouns or prepositions to denote the relevant person.

pronouncement story Short narrative passage in the gospels, built up around a pronouncement or saying of Jesus; e.g. Mk. 2.1–12, healing of the paralytic, or 2.23–8, plucking grain on the Sabbath. Essentially the same as an APOPHTHEGM or a PARADIGM, it is perhaps the most commonly used term of the three.

propitiation A placating (of God) for an offence committed; a non-biblical word, it should be replaced by EXPIATION.

proselyte In NT times, a convert to Judaism.

proskynesis (Greek) 'Reverence', 'worship'.

prosopon (Greek) 'Face', 'presence', 'person'.

prostaxis The use of the Hebrew *waw* or the Greek *kai* to mark the beginning of a clause or sentence, rather than as a conjunction.

pro tanto (Latin) Good as far as it goes, but not the last word.

protasis The 'if . . .' clause of a conditional sentence, the main clause being the APODOSIS.

Protevangelium (of James) Popular, legendary narrative of the birth and marriage of Mary, and the events surrounding the birth of Jesus; written, in Greek *c.* 140, for

115

the glorification of Mary, it had considerable influence on later works in the same genre and on the development of Mariology.

proto- First; as in *Protomartyr*, Stephen.

proto-apocalyptic Post-exilic prophetic literature, from about the 5th to the 3rd cent. BC, such as Is. 24–7, Joel 2 and Zech. 9–14, which has many of the literary characteristics of APOCALYPTIC writing with an overtly eschatological outlook, but in rather general terms that lacks the precise historical immediacy of a work such as Daniel.

proto-evangelium Occasional title for Gen. 3.15 (understood in a messianic light) in which the Lord promises Eve that her offspring will triumph over the serpent.

protohistory First history, between the prehistoric and historic periods – the 4th millenium BC, and the origin of writing.

Proto-Luke Supposed first draft of Luke's Gospel, before he had come across Mark, consisting of Q and L. (B. Streeter)

Proto-Massoretic Text The official text (textus receptus) of the Hebrew Bible, adopted by the Rabbis probably at the council of Jamnia, late 1st cent. AD, which became the basis for the later MASSORETIC TEXT.

Proto-Septuagint Another name for the OLD GREEK VERSION.

Proto-Theodotion Another name for the KAIGE RECENSION.

protreptic Literary work designed to exhort people to a particular philosophy or way of life; e.g. Wisdom of Solomon.

provenance Source or derivation.

Proverbs (Prov.) The classic example of WISDOM LITERATURE. Chs. 1–9, theological discourses on Wisdom, the latest section of the book, 5th cent. BC or perhaps even later; 10.1–22.16 and chs. 25–9, collections of couplets, probably from a school of Wisdom at Jerusalem from the reign of Solomon onwards; 22.17–24.22, the SAYINGS OF THE WISE; 30–1, four short collections, at least two of which are from Arabia.

Psalms (Ps./Pss.) The hymn book of the Jerusalem

Temple. Divided into five books, 1–41, 42–72, 73–89, 90–106, 107–150. Most scholars follow the numbering of the Hebrew text, but occasionally one encounters the Septuagint and Vulgate numbering which is usually one behind. Though some Psalms may be as early as the 12th cent. BC or as late as the 2nd, it is the post-exilic period that predominates.

Pseudepigrapha Various heterodox, and usually pseudonymous, Jewish works dating from the centuries immediately before and during the beginning of the Christian era, that are not included in the OT or Apocrypha. Repudiated by Rabbinic Judaism, many have been reworked by early Christian writers. As a category it has no precisely defined outlines.

pseudepigraphal Relating to works ascribed to someone other than the real author; e.g. Wisdom of Solomon, Gospel of Peter. In Jewish works a well-known figure from biblical history (but not later than Ezra) was usually chosen, in Christian works an Apostle. Every apocalyptic book except Revelation is pseudepigraphal.

Pseudo-Clementines Title of a Jewish-Christian corpus of writings of the 2nd and 3rd cent., comprising the CLEMENTINE HOMILIES, RECOGNITIONS and EPITOMES, with the KERYGMATA PETROU and the Acts of PETER, on which they were based.

Pseudo-Philo Name given to the author of BIBLICAL ANTIQUITIES.

psittacism Parrot-fashion repetition; automatic, unthinking response, a perennial tendency in worship.

psychologizing The improper use of psychological insights beyond what the biblical text can bear; or in more extreme cases the reduction of a text to a mere illustration of a theory of psychoanalysis; e.g. the construction of a personality profile from the Jacob stories, after one has accepted that they reflect not an individual's but a clan's history.

Q Name, derived from the German *Quelle* (Source), for the hypothetical written source of those passages, mainly sayings of Jesus, found in both Matthew and Luke but not Mark.

117

Where the hypothesis of a written sayings source is rejected, the texts are often referred to as Q *material*.

qahal (Hebrew) 'Assembly'. (Greek: EKKLESIA)

qal wahomer (Hebrew) Rabbinic principle of exegesis, equivalent to *a minore ad maius*, from the lesser to the greater, from the easier to the more difficult, which argues thus: 'If such-and-such be true, how much more must it be true that . . .'.

qere (Hebrew) 'What is read'. In the MASSORETIC TEXT of the Hebrew Bible, a correction, placed in the margin, of what is written (KETHIBH) in the text.

qere perpetuum A corrected reading that is always applicable to a particular word in the text, and is therefore not noted, the most important being ADONAI, which is always read for YHWH.

qinah (Hebrew) 'Lament', 'funeral dirge'.

qinah metre Characteristic verse metre of LAMENTA-TIONS, consisting of three stressed syllables in the first half of each distich, followed by two in the second.

Qoheleth (Hebrew) 'Preacher'. Alternative name for ECCLESIASTES.

Quelle See Q.

Quellenkritik (German) The analysis, criticism of sources behind a text.

quid pro quo (Latin) 'Something for something'; a favour for a favour.

quietist Relating to the religious attitude that urges the abandonment of human activity and the total self-surrender of the will to God.

Quinta An otherwise unknown Greek translation of the Hebrew OT, included at certain places in Origen's HEXAPLA as the fifth Greek version.

Qumran Texts See DEAD SEA SCROLLS.

Quo Vadis? (Latin) 'Whither goest thou?'. According to the Martyrdom of PETER, the words spoken by him as he fled from Rome and met Christ on the road, who answered, 'I am coming to be crucified again', whereupon Peter turned back and faced his martyrdom by being crucified upside down.

q.v./qq.v. (Latin: *quod vide*) 'Which see'; i.e. look up the entry/entries mentioned for further details.

R A biblical redactor who has combined or edited earlier source documents. In particular:

R^{JE} The pre-exilic editor from the Southern Kingdom who combined J and E, in the 7th cent. BC.

R^D The exilic editor who combined D and JE, in the 6th cent. BC.

R^P The post-exilic editor who combined all the earlier sources into the Pentateuch as we have it, using P as his framework, *c.* 400 BC.

Rabbinic Relating to the Jewish Rabbis, the sages and teachers of the 1st and 2nd cent. AD; it is therefore synonymous with TANNAITIC, though it is often used more generally.

Ras Shamra Texts Several hundred cuneiform tablets mainly in UGARITIC discovered in 1929 on the Syrian coast at the site of the ancient town of Ugarit. Dating mainly from the 14th cent. BC, they are a major source of information on Canaanite religion and mythology.

realized eschatology Technical term for the understanding that the aspects of the ESCHATON awaited by the OT prophets and their successors are no longer to be looked for in the future, but have been made present by the incarnation of Christ.

recapitulation The summing up of all things, in particular the long history of redemption, in Christ; Eph. 1.10.

recension A particular version of a text, whose transmission can be traced, following a revision of it by a later editor or copyist. In many contexts it is synonymous with TEXT-TYPE.

Recognitions See CLEMENTINE RECOGNITIONS.

recto (Latin) Front of a piece of paper or papyrus; opposite to *verso.*

redaction Editing, revising, arranging for publication.

redaction criticism The investigation of the editorial work done by biblical writers and compilers on earlier material. It is applicable to works such as the Synoptic Gospels or the Deuteronomic History which have identifiable sources within them, and asks what creative, theological role did the final author play in putting together and reworking the material before him.

Redaktionsgeschichte German for REDACTION CRITICISM.

119

Redeemer, Dialogue of the   See SAVIOUR, DIALOGUE OF THE.

Redenquelle   (German) 'Sayings source'.

redivivus   (Latin) 'Brought back to life'; e.g. the belief that Jesus was *Johannes Redivivus*, Lk. 9.7 & 19.

reductio ad absurdum   (Latin) Taking an argument to impractical, illogical lengths.

reductionism   Pejorative term for those theologies that seek to water down the traditional dogmas.

regula fidei   (Latin) 'Rule of faith'.

Regum, I–IV   Latin name of I & II SAMUEL and I & II KINGS.

Religionsgeschichtliche Schule   (German name) 'History of Religions School'. Group of late 19th early 20th cent. German biblical scholars, who laid stress on parallel texts and traditions within other religions and cultures.

Remnant, The   Those few whom the Lord will save from the promised destruction of Israel, who will form the core of the restored community; a major theme of the OT prophets.

resurgam   (Latin) 'I shall rise again'; a cry of defiant hope.

Revelation   (Rev.) The only APOCALYPTIC work in which the writer gives his own name, John, though not the author of the Gospel. Writing to the seven churches in western Asia Minor, he probably did so in the 60s in response to the persecutions under Nero, though another common date is the 90s in response to the Domitianic persecution. The Greek is sometimes so ungrammatical it appears deliberate.

rhetorical criticism   Study of the structural patterns, rhetorical devices and idioms used by an author in the creation of a literary text. A development from FORM CRITICISM, it places the emphasis on the style and technique of the individual writer, rather than on the shared and typical form or genre.

rib   (Hebrew) 'Lawsuit'. OT prophetic form in which the Lord issues his complaint against Israel for breaking his covenant; e.g. Jer. 2.4ff.

rigorism   In a general sense, a philosophy or theology that advocates extreme asceticism or the strictest adherence to the law.

Ritual Decalogue   Ex. 34.11–28. Set of thirteen, perhaps originally ten, commandments concerning Israel's worship.

ro'eh (Hebrew) 'Seer'. I Sam. 9.9, 'He who is now called a prophet was formerly called a seer.'

Romans (Rom.) Regarded as one of the later undisputed Pauline epistles, *c.* 58, written to that Church before he journeyed there, perhaps as an apologia of his gospel preaching.

Royalist Source There are (at least) two opposing views on the rise of the monarchy found in I Samuel, a *Royalist Source*, 9.1–10.16; 11, and an *Anti-Royalist Source*, 8; 10.17–27; 12. The Royalist Source is undoubtedly earlier; other than that no consensus exists as to their origin and development.

ruah (Hebrew) 'Breath', 'wind', 'spirit'. (Greek: *pneuma*)

Ruth (Rt.) Short story of great charm concerning Ruth, a Moabitess, who follows her mother-in-law to Bethlehem and marries Boaz, the great-grandfather of David. Generally reckoned to have been written in the 4th cent. BC against Ezra's stern ruling on marriage with foreign women, it has also been placed in the time of David, 10th cent. BC.

S (From *South* or *Seir*, the supposed place of origin) Early, non-Israelite source within Genesis. (R. Pfeiffer)

sacerdos (Latin) 'Priest'.

sacerdotium (Latin) 'Priesthood'.

Sache (German) 'Subject matter', and therefore the theological subject matter.

Sachexegese (German) 'Subject exegesis'. The investigation of the toal subject matter of a given text.

Sachhälfte (German) 'Subject half'; the meaning or teaching of a parable as opposed to the imagery (BILDHÄLFTE). It is a distinction rarely accepted, since it is precisely the inseparability of theme and imagery that is characteristic of a parable.

Sachkritik (German) 'Theological criticism'. (R. Bultmann)

Sahidic The most important dialect of COPTIC that had by the 4th cent. become the chief literary language of the whole Nile Valley, its style and spelling becoming largely standardized. The earliest version of the Bible dates from before AD 270.

Samaria, Ostraca of Several orders and receipts in Hebrew, for oil, wine and barley, from the reign of Jeroboam II

(786–746 BC), that throw light on the script, personal names etc. of the period.

Samaritan Pentateuch   The only part of the Hebrew Bible in the canon of the Samaritans, it followed a separate course of transmission from perhaps as early as the 3rd cent. BC; slightly divergent from the MASSORETIC TEXT, it often agrees with the SEPTUAGINT.

Sammler   (German) 'Collector', usually of two sources.

Samuel, I   (I Sam.) The story of Samuel, Saul and the early years of David, in particular the whole problem of the establishment of the monarchy for which there is both a ROYALIST and an Anti-Royalist Source.

Samuel, II   (II Sam.) Originally part of a single book with I Samuel. The story of the reign of David, including the main bulk of the SUCCESSION NARRATIVE, chs. 9–20.

Sanctum Sanctorum   (Latin) 'Holy of Holies'.

sapiential   Relating to the WISDOM LITERATURE.

sarx   (Greek) 'Flesh'.

Sätze heiligen Rechtes   (German) 'Sentences of holy law'. Suggested form of the earliest Christian law found in the NT, characterized by TALION and CHIASMUS; e.g. I Cor. 3.17, 'If anyone destroys the temple of God, God will destroy him'. (E. Käsemann)

Saviour, Dialogue of the   Gnostic gospel in the post-resurrection discourse genre, similar to SOPHIA JESU CHRISTI, which it follows in Codex III of the Nag Hammadi library.

Savoraim   Jewish scholars in the period after the completion of the Talmud, between the AMORAIM and the GEONIM.

Sayings of the Jewish Fathers   Less common title for the PIRQE ABOTH.

Sayings of the Wise   Title of what is probably the oldest section of PROVERBS, 22.17–24.22, based on the Wisdom of AMEN-EM-OPE.

sc.   (Latin: *scire licet*) 'One may understand'. Usually in quotations to introduce a more intelligible substitute, or fill in what was left as understood in the original.

scarab or **scaraboid**   Ancient, bettle-shaped seal.

Scheltrede   (German) '(Prophetic) accusation', 'reproach'.

scholia   Explanatory notes or commentary, inserted in the margins of ancient manuscripts; a Greek practice.

scriptio continua (Latin) Writing without any gaps between words or sentences; a characteristic of ancient manuscripts.

scriptorium Writing-room where scribes copied manuscripts.

Seder (Hebrew) 'Order', 'arrangement'. Used in rabbinic literature for (a) divisions in the lectionary; (b) the six sections of the Mishnah; (c) an order of prayer or worship. (Plural: *Sedarim*).

Seleucid Era Calendar reckoned from October 312 BC (though with some local variation), that became increasingly used throughout the eastern Mediterranean, until it became known as the *Grecian Age*.

seme A semantic unit; minimum element of meaning.

semeion (Greek) 'Sign'.

sememe The meanings of a MORPHEME; or a significant unit of meaning.

semiotics or **semiology** The study of signs. Closely related to STRUCTURALISM, it analyses not signs that lie behind a text and to which it may refer, but those inherent in the text itself, those that are encoded in the actual structure of its language.

Semitism or **Semiticism** Semitic (i.e. Hebrew or Aramaic) word or idiom within a, usually Greek, text.

Seneca and Paul, Letters of Set of fourteen apocryphal letters between the two great men, in which the Roman philosopher applauds the majesty of the Apostle's thought; probably written in the 3rd cent. to commend Christianity to the people of Italy.

Septima An otherwise unknown Greek translation of the Hebrew OT, included at certain places in Origen's HEXAPLA as the seventh Greek version.

Septuagint (LXX) The first and most important of the early Greek translations of the OT, made by Jews of Alexandria starting with the Torah in the 2nd cent. BC, and later covering the whole OT including the Apocrypha. It was the preferred translation of the early Church, and thus a major cause for the inclusion of the Apocrypha within the Christian canon of the OT.

Septuagintism Greek phrase characteristic of the SEPTUAGINT taken up by a NT writer.

Sermon on the Plain   Lk. 6.17–49. Shorter Lukan parallel to Matthew's *Sermon on the Mount*, chs. 5–7.

Servant Songs   Is. 42.1–4; 49.1–6; 50.4–11; 52.13–53.12. Four poems in Deutero-Isaiah that describe the SUFFERING SERVANT.

Sexta   An otherwise unknown Greek translation of the Hebrew OT, included at certain places in Origen's HEXAPLA as the sixth Greek version.

shaliach   (Hebrew) 'Messenger', 'apostle'.

shalom   (Hebrew) 'Peace'.

Shekinah   (Hebrew) 'Dwelling', 'resting'. The divine presence, the numinous immanence of God in the world. A non-biblical word used in rabbinic literature to avoid anthropomorphism.

Shema   Israel's confession of faith, Deut. 6.4: 'Hear O Israel, the LORD our God is the one LORD.'

Shemoneh-Esreh   See EIGHTEEN BENEDICTIONS.

Sheol   In the OT, the shadowy realm of departed spirits. (Greek: HADES)

Shepherd of Hermas   See HERMAS, SHEPHERD OF.

shewa   Particular dots under a Hebrew consonant denoting an ultra-short or non-existent vowel sound.

Sibylline Oracles   Collection of fifteen Jewish and Christian fictitious, poetic prophecies, based on the more well known pagan models; Greek, from the 2nd cent. BC to the 5th cent. AD.

sic   (Latin) 'Thus'; added (in brackets) after quoted words to draw attention to the fact that a misspelt or anomalous phrase is not the result of misquotation.

sich realisierende Eschatologie   (German) 'Eschatology in the process of being realized'. Common compromise between a future ESCHATOLOGY and a present REALIZED ESCHATOLOGY; the Kingdom of God has been inaugurated by Jesus and is therefore present, but it has yet to be fully realized and is therefore also future.

Siedlungsgeschichte   (German) 'History of sedentarization'; in particular the settling of the early Hebrews in Canaan.

sigillata   Pieces of pottery with the impressions of seals.

siglum   Character or letter used to denote a Bible manuscript or version; e.g. 'B' for Codex Vaticanus.

signans (Latin) 'Signifier'. The sign.

signatum (Latin) 'Signified'. The object to which the sign refers.

Signs Source or **Book of Signs** Hypothetical source document behind John's Gospel, containing the 'signs' described in chs. 2–11; see 20.30.

Siloam Inscription Hebrew inscription on stone, recording the digging of the water supply tunnel under Jerusalem in the reign of Hezekiah, *c.* 700 BC, II Kg. 20.20.

Similitudes of Enoch See I ENOCH.

Similitudes of Hermas See HERMAS, SHEPHERD OF.

sine die (Latin) 'Without a day (being named)'; indefinitely.

sine qua non (Latin) 'Without which not'. An indispensable condition.

Sinuhe, Story of Autobiographical account of an Egyptian official's exile to Asia and later return; 20th cent. BC.

Sippenethos (German) 'Clan ethic'; a possible nomadic source of Israelite law and wisdom.

Sirach (Sir.) Chs. 1–42.14, advice in the Proverbs tradition on all aspects of living; 42.15ff and 51.1ff, two hymns of praise; 44–50, eulogy of Hebrew ancestors. A compilation of late Wisdom teaching, written in Hebrew *c.* 190 BC, by Jesus ben Sira, a professional sage in Jerusalem, and translated into Greek by his grandson in 132 BC.

situation ethics Modern ethical approach that, seeing the limitations of moral laws, argues that each situation should be judged on its own merits, and that one should (as a Christian) be guided only by the gospel demand of love.

Sitz im Leben (German) 'Setting in life', referring to the circumstances in the life of a community in which a particular biblical story or saying was developed and understood.

sola fide (Latin) '(Justification) by faith alone'.

sola scriptura (Latin) 'Scripture alone' is the basis on which we are to judge the truth or worth of Christian doctrines.

solecism Violation of the rules of grammar or syntax.

Solomon, Annals of or **Book of the Acts of Solomon** Royal archives used in the Deuteronomic History; I Kg. 11.41.

Solomon, Odes of   Pseudepigraphal collection of 42 early, heterodox, Christian hymns; Greek or Syriac, 1st or 2nd cent. AD.

Solomon, Psalms of   Pseudepigraphal collection of 18 songs, that look to the coming of the Messiah; probably written by a Palestinian Pharisee, in Hebrew between 70 and 40 BC.

Solomon, Song of   (S. of S.) Beautifully erotic and graceful collection of love poems, with no overt religious connotations, sung by bride, bridegroom and chorus. Put together in the 3rd cent. BC from much earlier material.

Solomon, Wisdom of   See WISDOM, BOOK OF.

soma   (Greek) 'Body'.

Song of Songs   Another name for the Song of SOLOMON.

Sopherim   (Hebrew) 'Scribes'. Jewish teachers and exponents of the law, from the time of Ezra to the time of the Rabbis, who transmitted the biblical text and related traditions.

Sophia   (Greek) 'Wisdom', used especially when personified, as in Prov. 8.22ff. In Gnostic thought she becomes the first female emanation of the Highest God.

Sophia Jesu Christi   Gnostic gospel, originally in Greek from the late 2nd cent., in the post-resurrection discourse genre, and quite probably based on the *Epistle of Eugnostos the Blessed*, which immediately precedes it in Codex III of the Nag Hammadi library.

Sophonias   Latin form of the name ZEPHANIAH.

soteriology   That branch of theology that deals with the salvation of man worked by Jesus Christ.

spiration   God's creative act expressed in the act of breathing; e.g. Ezek. 37.6.

Sprachereignis   German for LANGUAGE EVENT.

sq./sqq.   (Latin) The next verse/verses, page/pages, etc.

Stammessage   (German) 'Tribal tales', of the early OT, in which the hero personifies a group or tribe rather than a historical individual.

statu quo ante, (in)   (Latin) 'In the state it was before'.

stele   (Occasionally *stela*) Ancient, upright, stone monument with an inscription.

stemma codicum   (Greek–Latin barbarism) Hypothetical

genealogical table of manuscripts showing the transmission of a text.

steno-symbol Sign or symbol that has a one-to-one relation to what it represents; e.g. the he-goat of Dan. 8.5 representing Alexander the Great. Distinguished from a TENSIVE SYMBOL.

stich A clause, or sometimes (and this is not always the same) a line, of poetry.

stichos (Greek) 'Line'. Average line in a written text; used in:

  stichometry Ancient means of measuring the contents of a manuscript, as a rough check on accuracy after copying.

stratigraphy Method of archaeological dating based on *strata*, the layers of earth and debris that have accumulated over the centuries, each layer containing fragments of pottery etc. characteristic of its period.

Streitgespräch German for CONTROVERSY DIALOGUE.

strophe (Hebrew poetry; plural: *strophes* or *strophae*) Series of lines of verse forming a unit that is then repeated; what in hymns we would call a *verse*.

structuralism and **structural analysis** Study of the biblical texts, strongly influenced by seminal thinkers in France such as Lévi-Strauss and Saussure, which seeks the structures common to all language that are encoded in any particular text. Using formal models from linguistics, Cartesian logic and anthropology, it brings out the signs and structures inherent in human thought, which are hidden behind the narratives. It does not seek the mind or intention of the writer, nor is it interested in any historical dimension, but rather faces the reader with the text itself, and gives him the means to analyse it in a manner common to any other text of any other culture.

Strukturmuster (German) 'Structural model'. In STRUCTURALISM, the equivalent of a GATTUNG.

Sub-Akhmimic Minor COPTIC dialect attested only in the 4th and 5th cent., but important for the large number of Gnostic texts written in it.

Sub-Apostolic Age Period following the APOSTOLIC AGE, after the completion of the NT; AD 90 to the mid-2nd cent.

subordinationism Theology of the Trinity that regards

the Son as subordinate to the Father, or less commonly, the Holy Spirit as subordinate to both.

sub specie aeternitatis   (Latin) 'In the context of eternity'. As it were the opposite of a SITZ IM LEBEN.

Succession Narrative   II Sam. (6–7), 9–20; I Kg. 1–2. 'Secular' historical account of the later years of David's reign and the political intrigues surrounding the succession to his throne; the 'world's first history' it probably dates from Solomon's reign.

Suffering Servant   Powerful, enigmatic figure described in the four SERVANT SONGS of Deutero-Isaiah, in whom the idea of expiatory suffering is first revealed. Called the 'Servant of the LORD' (Hebrew: *'Ebed YHWH*), his identity is furiously debated by scholars: at times he stands clearly for the nation of Israel, elsewhere he seems equally clearly to be an individual. His portrayal at least in part inspired by the suffering of Jeremiah, he was, for Christians, fulfilled in the person of Jesus.

Suicide, Dispute over   The dialogue of a man, who is weary of life, with his soul; an Egyptian text of the late 3rd millenium, often linked with Job.

sui generis   (Latin) 'Of its own kind'; unique, peculiar.

sui ipsius interpres   (Latin) 'Itself its own interpreter'. The interpretation of one passage of the Bible by reference to another; it was a major principle of the Reformers, using as point of reference Paul's teaching on justification by faith alone, which was for them the 'canon within the canon'.

Sumerian   Earliest known written language, of the 4th millenium from Mesopotamia, non-Semitic, non-Indo-European. Superseded by AKKADIAN, hence the umbrella term *Sumero-Akkadian*.

Sumerian King List   Mythical, historical list, *c.* 20th cent. BC, of kings and rulers from the time when 'kingship was first lowered from heaven'; their rule declines from 20 to 30,000 years before the Flood to more realistic numbers by the end of the text.

summun bonum   (Latin) 'The supreme good'.

suneidesis   (Greek) 'Conscience'.

supererogation   Doing more than duty requires.

supermundane   Belonging to a region above the earth.

Susanna and the Elders One of the later additions to Daniel, found as ch. 13 in the Septuagint and Vulgate or as a separate book of the Apocrypha. Written in the 1st or 2nd cent. BC, probably in Greek, it is an elegant little short story in the Wisdom tradition, in which the quick thinking of Daniel saves the beautiful Susanna from the two wicked elders.

s.v. (Latin: *sub voce*) 'Under the word'.

syllabary Dictionary for an ancient Near Eastern syllabically-written language.

syllepsis Use of a word to qualify two or more other words, while only agreeing grammatically with one; e.g. a masculine adjective used with two nouns, one masculine the other feminine.

Symmachus, Version of Readable and elegant Greek translation of the Hebrew OT, made in the late 2nd cent. AD by Symmachus, variously described as an Ebionite or a Samaritan who became a Jew; noted for the removal of anthropomorphisms.

symploce Literary style in which ANAPHORA and EPIPHORA are combined.

synaesthesia Figure of speech in which there is a metaphorical linking of two inappropriate terms; e.g. Ex. 5.21, 'You have made us stink in the eyes of Pharaoh' or Is. 2.1, 'The word which Isaiah . . . saw'.

Synaxarion A LECTIONARY for the secular, moveable year.

synaxis (Greek) 'Assembly for worship'.

synchronic (Greek) 'With time'. In relation to a language or a text, that which is static or is unconnected with any historical development; that which deals with the text as it is, and not with how it came to be. As opposed to DIACHRONIC.

syncope (Hebrew poetry) Contraction of a word by omitting a syllable, such as 'Yahweh' to 'Yah', Ps. 68.4. Also a cutting short or sudden interruption.

syncretism The attempt to combine different or opposite religious doctrines or practices; more especially the inclusion of pagan ideas and rituals into Judaism or Christianity.

synecdoche Figure of speech in which the part is used to refer to the whole, e.g. 'Jerusalem' for 'Judah', or the whole is used to refer to the part, e.g. 'the whole world' for 'all men'.

129

synergism Belief that the human will co-operates with divine grace to achieve the work of redemption.

synopsis Arrangement of the first three, or all four, of the gospels in parallel columns, so as to show clearly their shared subject matter and wording.

Synoptic Gospels Matthew, Mark and Luke, which share a large amount of common material, mostly in the same order.

Synoptic problem The question of the literary relationship between the three Synoptic Gospels, raised by the large number of parallel passages. This leads to such solutions as the TWO SOURCE and FOUR SOURCE HYPOTHESES, and the supposition of such works as Q, M, L, PROTO-LUKE etc.

syntagm In literary or structural analysis, the sentence or comparable literary unit, whether shorter or longer, characterized by a chain-like order and sequence of meaning.

syntagmatic relations The horizontal, linear, sequential or diachronic, relations within a text, as opposed to the PARADIGMATIC RELATIONS.

Syriac Dialect of Eastern ARAMAIC spoken by early Christians, that developed into the major literary language of the eastern Churches.

Syriac Vulgate Rare name for the PESHITTA.

Syrian Text Former name of the LUCIANIC TEXT.

Syro-Hexaplar Syriac translation of the SEPTUAGINT text contained in Origen's HEXAPLA; scholarly and accurate, it also preserves his critical symbols; AD 617.

syzygy In Gnostic thought, a pair of cosmological opposites, e.g. male and female.

tabula rasa (Latin) Clean sheet, blank page (figurative).

tachygraphy Art of quick writing; the use of CURSIVE handwriting or DEMOTIC SCRIPT etc.

Taheb (Samaritan) 'Restorer'. Prophetic figure who would return to restore the temple on Mount Gerizim and herald the messianic age.

talion Retaliation. See LEX TALIONIS.

Talmud (Hebrew) 'Study', 'learning'. Massive compilation of Jewish teaching, consisting of the MISHNAH and its commentary, the GEMARA. There are two versions:

Babylonian Talmud Completed at the end of the 5th cent.; some 2½ million words, it is the authoritative text.

Jerusalem (or **Palestinian**) **Talmud** Probably completed a century earlier, it is much shorter and never gained the same authority as the above.

Tanak Modern Jewish scholars' name for the Hebrew Bible, i.e. the OT, derived from the initial letters of *Torah*, *Nebiim* and *Ketubim*.

Tannaim The Jewish teachers, or Rabbis, of the 1st and 2nd cent. AD, from the time of Rabbi Hillel to the compilation of the MISHNAH. (Adjective: *tannaitic*)

targum Aramaic translation or paraphrase of the whole or part of the Hebrew Bible, when the latter was no longer a commonly spoken language. Originally written to follow the synagogue reading of Scripture, they included many interpretative additions. Dating such non-literary texts is difficult, but it seems certain that a targum or more probably several were widely used in 1st cent. AD Palestine, and must therefore have had some influence on the writing of the NT.

Taryag Hebrew mnemonic for the number 613 – the 613 precepts of the Torah, as codified by the early Scribes.

taxis (Greek) '(Literary or rhetorical) composition'.

Teacher of Righteousness Title given to the leader of the *Qumran* community in the mid-2nd cent. BC; possibly its founder, he certainly shaped its theology and structure, his authority remaining long after his death.

Teaching of the Twelve Apostles Former name, now rare, for the DIDACHE.

teleology Study of ends and final causes, or of the purpose for which things are designed.

tell (From the Arabic for 'hillock') An artificial mound, the result of accumulated debris over the centuries from an ancient city.

temenos (Greek) Sacred ground surrounding a shrine or temple.

Tendenzkritik (German; only partially translated to *Tendenz criticism*) Analysis of the particular intention, tendency or bias with which a biblical writer approaches his subject.

tensive symbol Symbol whose meaning cannot be adequately expressed by any one referent. For many this is a true symbol, as opposed to a STENO-SYMBOL which is only a sign. 'The Son of Man' is an example of something that begins as a tensive symbol, rich in meaning, and becomes a steno-symbol when it is used simply as another title for Jesus.

teratology Popular genre of literary narrative that delights in marvels and prodigies, examples being found in the apocryphal literature.

terminus ad quem (Latin) 'Limit to which'. The latest possible date that can be assigned to an event or a text.

terminus a quo (Latin) 'Limit from which'. The earliest possible date that can be assigned to an event or a text.

terminus post quem Occasional synonym for TERMINUS A QUO.

tertium quid (Latin) 'Some third thing'. A third unknown quantity related to, or developing from, two known quantities; or simply a point of comparison, *tertium comparationis*. If such a possibility cannot exist, the phrase is *tertium non datur*.

Testament of our Lord in Galilee Less common name for the EPISTULA APOSTOLORUM.

Testaments of the Twelve Patriarchs (Test. XII) Pseudepigraphal collection of prophecies and exhortations by each of the sons of Jacob built up around incidents from their lives. A rambling, untidy work, it does however contain much significant material particularly ethical teaching, but possible influence on Christianity is disputed: most probably it is a Greek Christian expansion and major reworking of earlier Hebrew texts. A date between 200 BC and AD 200 depends on one's conclusion.

Tetragrammaton Technical term for the four-lettered Hebrew name of God, YHWH, which from the late OT period onwards was regarded as too holy to be pronounced.

Tetrateuch Scholars' name for the first four books of the OT, Genesis–Numbers, compiled from the same three sources J, E and P (qq.v.).

textemes In structural analysis, a literary unit, generally larger than a sentence, that builds up the structure of particular types of texts or genres.

text immanent Relating to meaning or significance that is immediately obvious from the text itself, and does not require one to go behind it.

text-type   The largest grouping of Bible manuscripts put forward by text critics; showing a set of shared characteristics, largely the result of geography and major, local revision, which distinguishes that body of manuscripts from others. The main ones are ALEXANDRIAN, WESTERN and LUCIANIC.

textual criticism   Study of the Bible texts as they have been transmitted and altered by copyists, and the assessment of the value of different manuscripts, so as to discover what seem most probably to have been the precise words used by the author concerned. Its primary task is therefore the restoration of the original texts corrupted by centuries of being copied by hand.

Textus Receptus   (Latin) 'Received Text'. The Greek NT text of printed Bibles up to the critical editions of the 19th cent.; in Britian the edition used was that of Stephanus in 1550, on the continent that of Elzevir in 1633. In the OT the phrase is used (without capitals) for the PROTO-MASSORETIC TEXT.

thanatism   Belief that the soul ceases to exist after death.

thanatography   Account of someone's death; e.g. Deut. 34, of Moses.

thanatopsis   Meditation upon death.

thaumaturge   (Greek) 'Worker of miracles', 'wonder-worker'. Sometimes used by pagans as a pejorative title for Christ.

theandric   Relating to both God and man, especially in the person of Christ.

theanthropism   The union of God and man in Christ.

Thebaic   Former name of the SAHIDIC dialect of Coptic.

theios aner   (Greek) 'Divine man'. Hellenistic theme of the religious hero gifted with miraculous powers and divine qualities, the classic example being *Apollonius of Tyana* of the 1st cent. AD. Disputed influence on early Christianity.

theism   Belief in God, and so distinct from *atheism*; in one God, and so distinct from POLYTHEISM; in a transcedent God, separate from the created world, and so distinct from PANTHEISM; (generally) to the exclusion of any other possible God, and so distinct from HENOTHEISM; in a personal God, who cares for and governs those whom he has created, and so distinct from DEISM.

theocracy Government by God (through his representatives), as in pre-monarchical Israel, for whom Yahweh alone was king.

theocrasy Combination or annexation of various gods or divine attributes into a single God. Not to be confused with THEOCRACY.

theodicy The justification of God's ways to men, particularly his goodness, justice and power in the face of evil and suffering.

Theodotion, Version of 2nd cent. AD Greek version of the OT, very similar to the Septuagint, of which it may be a revision rather than a direct translation; used by the Church Fathers particularly for the text of Job and Jeremiah.

theogony Mythology concerning the birth of the gods.

theolepsy Possession or seizure of a person by the spirit of a god.

theologia perennis (Latin) The mainstream of Western (Catholic) theology.

theologoumenon A (merely) theological statement, as distinct from a revealed truth or a historically verifiable fact; e.g. the assertion that Moses wrote the books of the Pentateuch, an interpretation demanded neither by the texts themselves nor by divine revelation.

theomachy A striving against God; e.g. Jacob who wrestled all night with a 'man' at the river Jabbok, Gen. 32.24ff. Also, in pagan mythology, a war among the gods.

theomorphism Doctrine that man has the form and likeness of God, Gen. 1.26.

theonomy Ethical teaching that moral laws find their ultimate authority in the will of God.

theophany Act by which God manifests himself to man; e.g. at Mount Sinai, Ex. 19.16ff.

theophoric name One that contains 'god', or his name, within it; e.g. Elijah or Theophilus.

theopneust Divinely inspired.

theriolatry Worship of animals.

Thessalonians, I (I Th.) The earliest of Paul's letters, c. 51, and thus perhaps the earliest text of the NT, much concerned with the imminent second coming of Christ.

Thessalonians, II (II Th.) Probably written by Paul shortly after the first letter, taking up many of its points but with a different emphasis, or written by someone else to 'correct' the Pauline text.

theurgy Manipulation of a supernatural power by certain rites and formulae.

Thomas, Acts of Early 3rd cent. apocryphal Acts giving a colourful description of the Apostle's missionary activity in India; written in Syriac and clearly Gnostic in character. Contains the Hymn of the PEARL.

Thomas, Apocalypse of Short 4th cent. apocryphon, probably in Greek; based on Revelation, it outlines seven signs that will precede the end of the world.

Thomas, Gospel of Coptic text from Nag Hammadi of the 4th cent. AD, deriving from a Greek original of *c*. 150. A collection of 114 sayings of Jesus, very important despite obvious Gnostic additions for being close in form and content to the hypothetical sayings source Q (q.v.).

Thomas, Infancy Gospel of Legendary stories about Jesus between the ages of five and twelve years, later incorporated into other collections of infancy stories; probably in Greek, late 2nd cent. Apparently unconnected with the Gospel of Thomas.

Three Children, Song of the One of the later additions to the book of Daniel, consisting of the *Prayer of Azariah*, a plea for national deliverance, and a canticle of praise, known in Christian worship as the *Benedicite*. Found as a short book of the Apocrypha or interpolated after 3.23 in the Septuagint and Vulgate; probably written in Hebrew, 1st or 2nd cent. BC, for some other context. Since it is also known as the *Song of the Three Young Men*, it must be distinguished from the Story of the THREE YOUNG MEN.

Three Young Men, Story of the I Esd. 3.1–5.6. Popular story of a debating contest on what is the strongest thing on earth: wine, kings, women or truth; incorporated into his history by the writer of I Esdras.

Thronbesteigungsfest German for ENTHRONEMENT FESTIVAL.

Timothy, I & II (I & II Tim.) With Titus, they make up the *Pastoral Epistles*, almost certainly not written by Paul, but pseudonymously after his death by a disciple, perhaps making use of genuine Pauline passages. Much concerned with church administration and defence against false teaching, they are among the latest books of the NT, 90s?

tiqqune sopherim (Hebrew) 'Emendations of the scribes'. Minor alterations and euphemisms introduced into the Hebrew text of the OT by early scribes, before the Massoretic Text.

Titus (Tit.) See TIMOTHY, I & II.

Titus, Letter of Pseudo- Commendation of virginity extant in a single 8th cent. Latin manuscript; it is of interest for its extensive quotation from the apocryphal literature.

Tobit (Tob.) Wisdom story of about the 2nd cent. BC, with an angel, a demon, a miracle cure, romance, adventure, and the piety and morality of late OT Judaism. Ostensibly set in 8th cent. Nineveh, it is in part based on the Wisdom of AHIKAR.

todah (Hebrew) 'Thanksgiving'.

toledoth (Hebrew) 'Generations', in particular of the formula in Genesis 'These are the generations of . . .', 2.4 and *passim*, which serves to give the book a unified framework.

toparch Petty king or prince of a small district.

toponymy Study of the place-names of a country, as indicators of who settled and lived there in the past.

Torah (Hebrew) 'Teaching', 'instruction', but most often translated 'law'. Used in a wide range of contexts, it can refer to the whole or almost any part of the divine revelation, or its collection and transmission by men. However, as a title it is most often given to the *Pentateuch*.

Tosephta Collection of TANNAITIC traditions that very largely parallels the MISHNAH; also written in Hebrew at much the same time, it seems in parts to be directly dependent upon it, though in all it is some four times longer, with a higher proportion of HAGGADAH.

totemism Primitive belief that a person or a tribe is associated with a species of plant or animal; e.g. Leah – wild cow? Rachel – ewe?

tractate Usually for a book or section of the TALMUD.

tradent A person, or community, who transmits the sacred tradition.

traditio (Latin) 'Tradition': the process of transmission.

traditio-historical criticism Study of the transmission of traditions within the life of the community from which they came, before, during and after their incorporation into oral and written forms. Used primarily of the OT, in which the process of transmission is that much longer, it takes up the investigation from where FORM CRITICISM leaves off, being interested in the complete history and background of the relevant Israelite institutions, rather than simply the texts themselves. However of all the 'criticisms' it is probably the most difficult to define precisely, for its scope can, depending on the scholar, be exceedingly broad. (German: ÜBER-LIEFERUNGSGESCHICHTE)

Traditionsgeschichte (German) 'Tradition history' Though some scholars make precise distinctions, it is in general a less common synonym for ÜBERLIEFERUNGSGES-CHICHTE.

traditum (Latin) 'Tradition': that which is transmitted.

traducianism Doctrine that the soul is generated with the body. Contrary to CREATIONISM.

transcendence The character of God whereby he utterly surpasses, stands above and remains independent of his created world. Contrasted with IMMANENCE.

trichotomy Division into three; more especially the ancient division of man into body, mind and spirit.

tricolon or **tricola** More commonly called a TRISTICH.

triple tradition Material common to all three Synoptic Gospels.

trisagion Greek title for the 'Holy, Holy, Holy' of Is. 6.3.

tristich (Hebrew poetry) Three line unit of verse, one line longer than the more common DISTICH. Occasionally called a *tricolon* or *tricola.*

tritheism Mistaken approach to the Trinity that sees the three persons but not the unity. Mohammed had this problem.

Trito-Isaiah Isaiah chs. 56–66. Written perhaps by more than one writer, in Palestine in the early years of the restoration, 530–500 BC, it follows many of the ideas of 1st and 2nd Isaiah, but with a greater concern for the true character of worship.

Trito-Zechariah Zechariah chs. 12–14. See DEUTERO-ZECHARIAH.

trochee (Hebrew poetry) Verse metre of one stressed syllable followed by one unstressed. (Adjective: *trochaic*)
trope A figure of speech, such as metaphor, metonymy, etc.
tropological interpretation Ancient form of exegesis that sought the moral, ethical meaning of the text.
Truth, Gospel of Coptic treatise from Nag Hammadi. Probably written by the Gnostic Valentinus, in Greek *c.* 150, it is rather more a sermon than a gospel, unfolding the significance of Christ's mission as the Word and Name of the Father.
Tugendkatalog (German) 'Catalogue of virtues'; a literary device used in ethical teaching of the NT period; e.g. Gal. 5.22. Opposite of a LASTERKATALOG.
Twelve, Book of the The twelve Minor Prophets, Hosea–Malachi, when regarded as a single literary unit.
Twelve Patriarchs, Testaments of the See TESTAMENTS OF THE TWELVE PATRIARCHS.
Two Brothers, Tale of Egyptian tale of about the 13th cent. BC, in which a married woman tries to seduce a young, unmarried man and is rejected, comparable to Potiphar's wife with Joseph, Gen. 39.
two source hypothesis Perhaps the simplest and most common basic solution to the SYNOPTIC PROBLEM, namely that Matthew and Luke both independently used two sources when compiling their works, the Gospel of Mark and the sayings collection 'Q'.
Two Ways See DUAE VIAE.
typology Form of biblical exegesis found in NT writers that saw in many of the OT characters *types* or foreshadowings of Christ; e.g. Rom. 5.14, '. . . Adam who was a type of the one to come', or Heb. 7, Melchizedek foreshadows Christ's priestly office. By extension it can include events; e.g. I Pet. 3.20f, Noah in his Ark foreshadows baptism.

Überlieferungsgeschichte (German) 'History of the transmission of tradition' or TRADITIO-HISTORICAL CRITICISM.
ubiquity The divine omnipresence of the body of the risen Christ.

Ugaritic Cuneiform, alphabetic language, related to, and often identified with, CANAANITE, found in tablets from Ugarit (see RAS SHAMRA TEXTS), dated around the 14th cent. BC.

uncials Greek manuscripts of the Bible written in large, separate, capital letters; of vellum or parchment, they occur from the 3rd to the 8th cent., until superseded by MINUSCULES. The·most important Bible manuscripts are in this class (see under CODEX).

unction Anointing with oil in a religious context, usually for healing; Jas. 5.14.

universalism (1) Preaching of the later Hebrew prophets, such as Deutero-Isaiah, that God's love is not limited to Israel but embraces Gentiles as well.

(2) Doctrine that Hell is only temporary and that ultimately all men will be saved. (Greek: APOCATASTASIS)

Unknown Gospel See EGERTON PAPYRUS.

unpointed text Hebrew text, as in OT times, without VOWEL POINTS.

Ur- German prefix meaning 'primitive, original, earliest'.

Urdeuteronomium Supposed first draft of Deuteronomy, essentially restricted to chs. 12–26, being the copy presented to King Josiah at Jerusalem in 621 BC.

Urevangelium The ever elusive, original, Aramaic gospel that lies behind all others. First suggested at the end of the 18th cent. the search for it has now generally been abandoned.

Urgemeinde The earliest (Christian) community.

Urmarcus Supposed early, lost draft of Mark's Gospel.

Urmensch The primal or heavenly man.

Ur-Nammu, Laws of Oldest known law code, CASUISTIC in character, in Sumerian from the 21st cent. BC, of Ur-Nammu founder of the 3rd Dynasty of Ur.

Ursprach Hypothetical primitive language.

Urzeit The (non-historical) primeval period, of the early chapters of Genesis.

v./vv. Verse/verses.

variae lectiones (Latin) 'Variant readings'.

vaticinatio ex eventu or **vaticinatio post eventum** or

vaticinium ex eventu or **vaticinium post eventum**
Four Latin phrases meaning very much the same thing: a
prophecy or prediction made after the event.

Vergegenwärtigung (German   hermeneutical   term)
'Actualization', 're-presentation': making an ancient biblical text
or tradition real and accessible to the contemporary world.

verso   (Latin) Reverse side or back of a piece of paper or
papyrus; opposite to *recto*.

vetus   (Latin) 'Old' – usually in names.

v.i.   (Latin: *vide infra*) 'See below'.

via negativa   See APOPHATIC THEOLOGY.

viz.   (Latin: *videlicet*) 'Namely'.

vocalic   (Hebrew poetry) Rich in vowels.

Volksspruch   (German) 'Folk saying'. A popular proverb,
as opposed to an artistic saying of a professional sage
(KUNSTSPRUCH); coming from oral, non-literary tradition,
any example in the OT can, of course, be disputed.

Vorlage   (German) 'Model', 'prototype'. The particular
copy or recension of a work used as a source by someone
else.

Vorverständnis   (German)   'Pre-understanding',   with
which a reader approaches a text.

vowel points   Dots and dashes added above, below and
alongside Hebrew letters, by later scribes from around the
6th to the 10th cent. AD, to make good the absence of vowel
letters in that script.

v.s.   (Latin: *vide supra*) 'See above'.

Vulgate   Latin translation of the Bible by Jerome, late 4th
cent. AD; the most widely used version in the West.

wadi   (Arabic) Ravine or valley that is dry except in the
rainy season.

War Scroll   (1QM) Apocalyptic manual from Qumran for
the coming Holy War between the Sons of Light and the
Sons of Darkness; second half of the 1st cent. BC.

Wars of the Lord, Book of the   Lost, early Hebrew poetic
source, cited in Num. 21.14.

Weltanschauung   (German) 'A (comprehensive) view of
the world'.

'We' Passages of Acts   Where Luke uses the first person

140

plural in his account of Paul's journeys: Acts 16.10–17; 20.5–15; 21.1–18; 27.1–28.16.

Western non-interpolations Omissions found in the Greek NT text of Codex Bezae, significant because its general tendency is towards expansion.

Western Text An early form of the Greek NT, important because it is apparently unrevised; found mainly in manuscripts of the West, the chief witness is Codex Bezae.

wie es eigentlich geschehen ist (German) '(History) as it actually happened'.

Wirkungsgeschichte (German) 'History of effects'. The study of the impact that a text has had.

Wisdom, Book of (Wis.) Chs. 1–9, reflection on the nature of Wisdom; 10–19, review of the part played by Wisdom in the history of the Exodus, with (13–15) an attack on idolatry; written in Greek, and ascribed to Solomon, by an Alexandrian Jew, mid-1st cent. BC.

Wisdom literature A broad and necessarily imprecise term, it can be roughly divided into three categories. The classic and earliest form is the proverb, found in the Book of PROVERBS, or as developed later into more comprehensive teaching about how to act in life, in SIRACH and the Book of WISDOM; the attempt, in the post-exilic period, to understand and explain the presence of evil and suffering in the world, thus JOB, ECCLESIASTES and some of the Psalms; then there is the moralistic and entertaining story, such as the JOSEPH STORY, TOBIT and the first part of and additions to DANIEL.

In one sentence, Wisdom seeks to understand and master the world we live in. Often without any explicit concern for theology, it was an 'international' type of literature and only gradually became absorbed and influenced by Yahwism; its formal origins are from Egypt in the reign of Solomon, its importance increasing in the last centuries BC till it reaches its masterpiece (if that is not too facetious a title) in the Sermon on the Mount.

Woraufhin (German) 'Direction of inquiry', that determines the nature of the questions one will ask of a text.

word event Synonym for LANGUAGE EVENT.

Wortgeschehen German for WORD EVENT.

Writings, The Unless otherwise qualified, the literal translation of the Hebrew KETUBIM, the title of the third section of the OT. Often preferred to the older title, HAGIOGRAPHA.

yadah (Hebrew) 'Praise', 'thanksgiving', 'confession'.
Yahwism The faith of ancient Israel, from the time of Moses c. 1250 BC to the time of Ezra c. 400 BC, after which it is called *Judaism*.
Yahwist Name given to the unknown author or authors of J (q.v.).
YHWH The four-lettered Hebrew name of God, referred to as the *Tetragrammaton*. It is now commonly written by Christians 'Yahweh', replacing the older 'Jehovah', though in most Bibles out of respect for the ancient tradition that the name is too holy to be pronounced, it is written 'LORD'.

Zadokite Work Earlier name for the DAMASCUS DOCUMENT.
Zechariah (Zech.) Chs. 1–8, a series of night-visions from 520–518 BC, in which the prophet follows the same theme as HAGGAI, outlining more fully the character of the messianic age to come. For chs. 9–14, not from the prophet, see DEUTERO-ZECHARIAH.
Zephaniah (Zeph.) A Jerusalem prophet of c. 630 BC. Ch. 1, judgement upon Judah; 2, judgement upon the nations; 3, consolation to those who wait patiently for the Lord.
Zephaniah, Apocalypse of Lost Jewish apocryphon that may have been the basis for a Christian work of the same name, known from a 5th cent. Coptic papyrus.
zeugma Use of a word to qualify two or more seemingly disparate words in the same sentence.
ziggurat Ancient Mesopotamian temple tower built in steps and often of awesome size. Note the Tower of Babel, Gen. 11.
zikkaron (Hebrew) 'Memorial', 'remembrance', especially of the Exodus in the Passover festival. (Greek: ANAMNESIS)
Zion Gospel Edition An edition of the gospels, from Jerusalem perhaps as early as the 4th cent., which gives variant readings to Matthew from a 'Jewish Gospel', probably the Gospel of the Nazarenes.

zoism Belief that life depends on a peculiar vital principle, a life-force.

Zoroastrianism Religious system ascribed to Zoroaster (Zarathustra) in the early 6th cent. BC in Persia; noted particularly for its dualism, that may have influenced apocalyptic Judaism.

Zweiquellentheorie German for TWO SOURCE HYPOTHESIS.

Final Word

I am aware that in trying to help prospective students and interested amateurs through the complexities of biblical scholarship, I may only be adding to the sense of panic by listing such a bewildering array of unknown words. Do remember that the glossary is for reference only; you do not need to learn all these terms. Indeed, it probably would not do your brain much good to know any more than about half of them – unless you want to earn your money by them.

Still more important, do not set out to use any and every word contained here. Some of them must be of dubious quality and meaning for all their academic pedigree. If it is of any encouragement, I remain unconvinced that there is any real difference between form criticism and traditio-historical criticism. For all the hours of discussion. A moment's reflection is enough to remind one that the goal is to understand not the jargon but the Bible itself. All but the most humanist of theologians would concede that the best exegesis is by the grace of God.

The aim of this little book has not been to teach, but to enable you to become sufficiently familiar with the terminology of scholarly argument to learn from it and participate in it. Given time you too may approach that state of cheerful scepticism where true wisdom is reflected in the phrase, 'I really don't know . . .'.